Topics in Intraabdominal Surgical Infection

Edited by
Richard L. Simmons, M.D.
Professor of Surgery and Microbiology
University of Minnesota
Minneapolis, Minnesota

APPLETON-CENTURY-CROFTS/Norwalk, Connecticut

Prentice-Hall International, Inc., London
Prentice-Hall of Australia, Pty. Ltd., Sydney
Prentice-Hall of India Private Limited, New Delhi
Prentice-Hall of Japan, Inc., Tokyo
Prentice-Hall of Southeast Asia (Pte.) Ltd., Singapore
Whitehall Books Ltd., Wellington, New Zealand

ISBN: 0-8385-8958-8 (paperback)
ISBN: 0-8385-8959-6 (hardbound)

Cover and text design: Lucinda C. Carbuto

PRINTED IN THE UNITED STATES OF AMERICA

Contributors

David H. Ahrenholz, M.D.
Chief Resident in Surgery
University of Minnesota Hospitals
Minneapolis, Minnesota

John G. Bartlett, M.D.
Professor of Medicine
Chief, Infectious Disease Division
The Johns Hopkins Hospital
Baltimore, Maryland

H. Stephen Bjornson, M.D., Ph.D.
Associate Director
Surgical Infectious Disease Section
Department of Surgery
University of Cincinnati
College of Medicine
Cincinnati, Ohio

Thomas K. Hunt, M.D.
Professor of Surgery, Ambulatory and Community Medicine
University of California
San Francisco, California

Ronald Lee Nichols, M.D.
Henderson Professor of Surgery
Professor of Microbiology
Tulane Medical School
New Orleans, Louisiana

Richard L. Simmons, M.D.
Professor of Surgery and Microbiology
University of Minnesota
Minneapolis, Minnesota

H. Harlan Stone, M.D.
Professor of Surgery
Emory University School of Medicine
Atlanta, Georgia

Contents

Introduction

The six papers in this symposium represent formalizations of informal presentations presented in a symposium on October 1981 in San Francisco, California. The occasion was the first Searle Symposium on Intraabdominal Infections held in conjunction with the Annual Congress of the American College of Surgeons. So many members and guests of the American College of Surgeons registered for this symposium, that the program had to be repeated in the afternoon. This participation reflects the great concern this problem elicits in the community of practicing surgeons. Hopefully, the five contributions published herein will help to clarify some controversial issues and even crystalize questions to be pursued at subsequent symposia.

All of the contributors have spent their professional lives investigating the causes and cure of these severe, frequent and lethal problems. At one time or another, all have worked with animal models of intraperitoneal infection. All of the contributions in some way focus on the pathogenesis and treatment of mixed and synergistic infections in which both aerobic and anaerobic bacteria conspire to produce an infection in the closed intraperitoneal cavity. Dr. Simmons focuses on the host defenses which normally can be mobilized to deal with small intraperitoneal bacterial inocula. His investigations have been directed toward determining what the surgeon can do to minimize the surgical insult and aid the host defense. Drs. Nichols and Stone have focused on different aspects of the surgical care of the patient with intraperitoneal infection. Dr. Bjornson focuses on the basic science aspects of synergistic infections and their interaction with host defenses, and Dr. Bartlett discusses the antibiotic choices that can be made, both correct and incorrect, in antibiotic adjunctive therapy of this disease. Dr. Hunt gets to the root of many intraabdominal infections in the failure of enteric anastomosis to heal.

This symposium will hopefully supplement in some way the more complete and systematic treatment of these diseases in recent monographs:

Wilson, S.E., Finegold, S.M., Williams, R.A., (eds.), *Intra-Abdominal Infection*, McGraw-Hill Book Company, New York, 1982.

Simmons, R.L., Howard, R. (eds.), *Surgical Infectious Diseases*, Appleton-Century-Crofts, New York, 1982.

CHAPTER ONE

Therapeutic Principles in Peritonitis

Richard L. Simmons, M.D.
David H. Ahrenholz, M.D.

Secondary bacterial peritonitis does not simply result from bacterial contamination of the peritoneal cavity. In addition to the bacteria, certain adjuvant substances must overcome the local host defenses in order to establish the infectious process. Successful treatment of peritonitis requires rapid and permanent removal of both pathogen and adjuvant by mechanical means or by appropriate antimicrobial agents. Since Steinberg's comprehensive studies appeared in 1944,[1] few investigators have concentrated in this field. The present review is an update of a series of reviews[2,3] based on our own research and that of others on the biologic principles of peritonitis.

There are two types of peritonitis. The first type, primary peritonitis is probably the result of hematogenous spread to the peritoneal cavity from a distant site. A single species of bacteria is usually found—streptococci, pneumococci, gram-negative bacteria, or *Mycobacterium tuberculosis*. Secondary peritonitis, in contrast, usually arises because of injuries to or lesions of the gastrointestinal or genitourinary tract; typically, polymicrobial flora are found.

The number of deaths caused by peritonitis is significantly influenced by the source of the infection, the age of the patient, and the status of his or her immunologic defense system. When peritonitis originates from the small bowel (usually because of strangulation or obstruction), it can kill about 20% to 25% of the time.[3,4] When it results from a perforated duodenal or gastric ulcer,

1

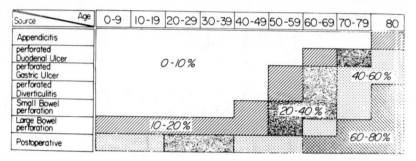

FIG. 1. Estimated mortality from peritonitis arranged according to age of patient and level of gastrointestinal tract perforation. (Ahrenholz DH, Simmons RL: Peritonitis and other intraabdominal infections. Chapter 34 in Surgical Infectious Diseases, RL Simmons, RL Howard (eds.), Appleton-Century-Crofts, 1982, p. 795.)

it has a mortality of about 5% to 10%.[4] The incidence of death after perforating appendicitis[3,5] ranges from 0% to 4%.[6,7] The mortality from perforations of the large bowel is about 20%;[8-10] about 40% of patients with a freely perforated diverticulum and 6% of those with abscesses[9] die; a mortality of 30% among cases of free perforation of colon carcinoma has been reported.[10]

Nearly half of all patients who are over 70 years of age die from all forms of secondary peritonitis, except appendicitis. Only 10% of patients under the age of 50 die under the same circumstances.

Renal insufficiency in patients with advanced diffuse peritonitis can increase the mortality by nearly 20%.[12] Over a 5-year period,[3] 42 (88%) of the patients who were referred to our hospital for hemodialysis to treat renal failu. ` and intraperitoneal sepsis died, despite the additional renal support.

Figure 1 illustrates an attempt to establish broad, prognostic categories based on the patient's age and the cause of the perforation (omitting other prognostic factors). It has been suggested that quantitative bacterial counts be used in diffuse peritonitis, because they correlate with prognosis. A classification system based on comparable prognoses must be established before the controversies about peritoneal diseases can be resolved.

PHYSIOLOGY OF THE PERITONEAL CAVITY

Although in a normal adult, the surface area of the peritoneal membrane (1.7 m²) approximates the total body surface area, the functional exchange surface of the peritoneum is smaller (less than 1.0 m^2) probably the result of variations in blood supply.[13] The peritoneal membrane acts as a passive, semipermeable barrier to the bidirectional diffusion of water and most solutes.

The peritoneal cavity is a potential space that normally contains a few milliliters of sterile fluid to provide lubrication for the abdominal viscera. The process of inflammation in peritonitis causes a rapid outpouring of fluid from the vascular and interstitial spaces into the peritoneal cavity to cause hypotension and sometimes death. This fluid shift can be potentiated by specific chemical factors such as pancreatic enzymes, bile, or gastric acid. Because of this fluid shift, diffuse peritonitis can be regarded as equivalent to burns over 50% of the body. For this reason, one of the burn formulas can be used to initiate fluid replacement. Blood pressure, central venous pressure, hematocrit, urine volume and concentration, and pulmonary artery wedge pressure are the most reliable indicators of the specific fluid requirements of each patient.

Lymphatic drainage of the peritoneal cavity is important in removing bacteria and other particles. The lymphatic vessels underlie the mesothelium only in the area of the diaphragm. Passive stretching of the diaphragm (as during exhalation) causes a rapid influx of fluid into the diaphragmatic lymphatics. Contraction of the diaphragmatic muscle during inhalation milks the contents into the efferent ducts. A simultaneous decrease in intrathoracic pressure with inhalation assists the cephalad lymph flow.

Particulate material less than 10 μM in diameter, including red cells and bacteria, can easily be cleared from the peritoneal cavity via stomata (8–12 μM in diameter) between the mesothelium cells which lie over these diaphragmatic lymphatics (Figure 2). Bacteria injected into the peritoneal space can be recovered from thoracic lymph within six minutes and from blood within 12 minutes. The discovery of this absorption into the systemic circulation was made before antibiotics were available and strongly influenced therapeutic thinking to prevent this contamination of the bloodstream.[14,15] In 1900, Fowler[15] introduced the semiupright position to prevent the rapid absorption of "toxins" from the peritoneal cavity in nine patients with peritonitis, and all survived. In 1944, it was reported that dogs that received intraperitoneal injections of bacteria, and kept in the upright position, had a delayed appearance of bacteria in the lymph. Absorption of bacteria was more rapid in the head-down position.[1]

Increased intraperitoneal pressure accelerates the clearance of material from the peritoneal cavity; conversely, depression of spontaneous respiration by general anesthetics decreases this clearance

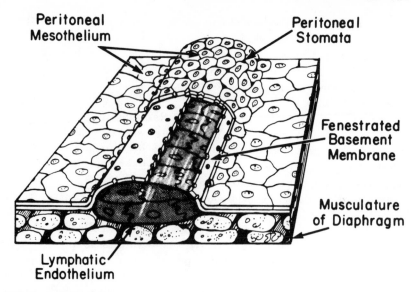

FIG. 2. Lymphatic lacunae on the peritoneal surface of the diaphragm. As can be seen, the mesothelial cells are flattened and polygonal everywhere except over the lymphatics, where they are smaller with stomata between the cells. These stomata correspond to fenestrations of the underlying basement membrane. The lymphatic endothelium lines the lymphatic channel and it probably communicates with the peritoneal cavity through the stomata.

in proportion to the decrease in the respiratory rate. On the other hand, high concentrations of CO_2 in inspired air will increase both the respiratory rate and the particle clearance from the peritoneal cavity.[16]

The absorption of fluid through the diaphragmatic lymphatics leads to a cephalad flow of peritoneal fluid (Figure 3A). Downward gravitational displacement of the liver increases the flow, creating a space into which peritoneal fluid is pulled. Respiratory cycles accelerate fluid absorption, and intestinal motility shifts material into the lateral peritoneal gutters and into an upward stream.

Until the recent past, most surgeons ignored the existence of intraperitoneal circulation. In a 1964 study, contrast material was injected into the abdominal cavities of patients after a routine appendectomy or a cholecystectomy. A pattern of circulation similar to that shown in Figure 3A defined more common routes of the spread of contaminated materials from a ruptured viscus. This pattern coincides with that of abscess localization after peritonitis in humans (Figure 3B) and demonstrates the upward movement of material into the subphrenic space.

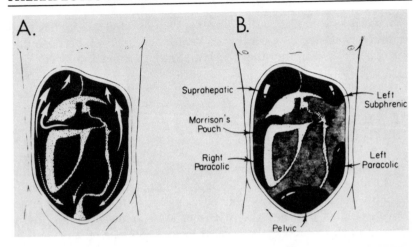

FIG. 3. A. Fluid circulation in the peritoneal cavity. The solid arrows illustrate the flow generated by diaphragmatic movement and the absorption of material from the diaphragmatic lymphatics. The dashed arrows indicate the effect of gravity in the upright position. (Adapted from Autio V: Acta Chir Scand (suppl) 321, 1964, with permission.) **B.** The sites of abscess formation in the peritoneal cavity. The labelled sites are most commonly involved, while the shaded areas are involved less commonly. (Adapted from Altemeier WA, et al.: Ann Surg 125:70, 1973, with permission.)

The Fowler position can often localize heavy material in a patient's pelvis and other dependent areas. This position also causes the subdiaphragmatic space to enlarge so that volume is increased and absorption decreased. The Fowler position may actually encourage the formation of pelvic and subdiaphragmatic abscesses. When the patient is in a flat or even in a head-down position, the pull of gravity may accelerate removal of particulate material from the peritoneal cavity by translymphatic diaphragmatic absorption. Fowler's position was the best treatment available for peritonitis until antibiotics and modern operative techniques were developed. Although the position contributed to abscess formation, abscesses were preferable to septicemia. After properly performed surgery, however, the clearance of residual intraperitoneal bacteria should be accelerated rather than deliberately delayed. Fowler's position, therefore, probably has little current applicability and may actually be detrimental. We have increased the survival rate of rats, with experimental *Escherichia coli* peritonitis, by maintaining them in the head-down position for a few hours immediately after intraperitoneal contamination (unpublished data). Conversely, the incidence of death was increased by using the head-up position.

Bacterial clearance will probably be impaired when positive-pressure, mechanically controlled ventilation is used, because diaphragmatic motion and thoracic lymphatic flow are impaired.

MESOTHELIAL INJURY AND PERITONEAL DEFENSES

The normal mesothelium is very sensitive; even exposure to saline for 30 minutes can cause it to be desquamated.[18] This sensitivity probably reflects an important peritoneal defense mechanism because injury of the mesothelium is usually followed by the laying down of fibrin, which seals visceral leaks and walls off the contaminated regions of the peritoneal cavity.

Fibrinous adhesions are normally removed from the peritoneal cavity by fibrinolysis. Although regenerating mesothelium has enhanced fibrinolytic properties,[18] injury including bacterial peritonitis, will temporarily depress its fibrinolytic activity.[19,20] Depressed fibrinolytic activity will result in the persistence of fibrinous adhesions until fibroblasts can lay down collagen, which leads to fibrous adhesions. Fresh blood will also encourage the growth of adhesions (Figure 4), probably by increasing the quantity of fibrin[21] produced.

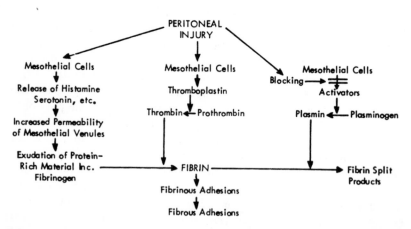

FIG. 4. Diagram of the events believed to lead to the formation of adhesions. (Adapted from Hau T, et al.: Surg Gynecol Obstet 148:415, 1979, with permission.)

Although effective experimentally,[22-24] anticoagulants and fibrinolytic agents have not been effective clinically in the reduction of the number of adhesions because of the incidence of postoperative bleeding.

HOST RESPONSE TO PERITONITIS

Serial bacterial counts, performed after the injection of a pure culture of E. coli into the peritoneal cavity of animals, indicate that the organisms are rapidly cleared. This "first-line" of defense begins even before the influx of neutrophils.[25] Unaltered bacteria appear in the diaphragmatic lymphatics within six minutes,[1] which suggests that the peritoneum's primary defense is its capacity to absorb bacteria through the regional lymphatic circulation. Bacteria are then filtered out by the thoracic lymph nodes or passed into the systemic circulation from which fixed tissue macrophages in liver, spleen, and lung can engulf and kill the bacteria. Humoral opsonins, in the form of natural antibodies and serum complement, bind to the bacterial surface to aid the process of phagocytosis.

Additionally, the peritoneum has a "second-line" of defense—the exudation of plasma containing opsonins, polymorphonuclear leukocytes, and macrophages into the peritoneal cavity so that intraperitoneal bacterial phagocytosis and destruction can take place (Figure 5). The inflammatory exudate is initiated by several stimuli: (1) the chemical irritation of the intestinal contents themselves, (2) the interaction between the lipopolysaccharide surface coating of the enteric bacteria and the serum complement with the activation complement cascade. The products of this cascade consist of vasoactive and chemotactic factors which can amplify the inflammatory response.

By releasing quantities of fibrin-containing fluid, the peritoneal cavity can isolate the infected material into localized pockets and seal small perforations. This newly formed fibrin network can also isolate the process further by joining adjacent peritoneal surfaces. Peritonitis eliminates the fibrinolytic activity of the mesothelium and stabilizes the loculation. The protective properties of the omentum in sealing intestinal perforations are due to its freedom to move in response to the adhesive fibrin exudates.

Adhesions would probably not localize infections or seal leaks if the bowel had normal motility. A state of local paralysis and rigidity

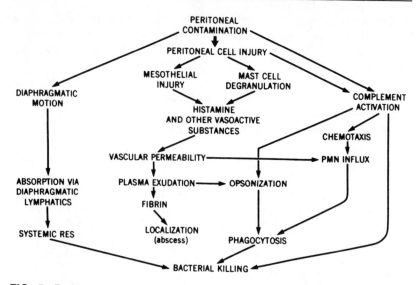

FIG. 5. Peritoneal response to contamination. Diaphragmatic motion is the principal means of systemic absorption of peritoneal contents. The influx of phagocytic cells kills the bacteria in situ. Fibrin deposits tend to wall off the process but interfere with clearance and phagocytosis, often resulting in an abscess. (From Ahrenholz DH, Simmons RL: Chapter 34 in Surgical Infectious Diseases, RL Simmons and RJ Howard (eds.), Appleton-Century-Crofts, 1982, p. 795.)

of both the diaphragmatic and abdominal wall muscles result from the inflammation and irritation around the intestine.[26] The result is better loculations of the inflammatory effusions. The abdominal rigidity further inhibits respiration and the absorption of toxic material.

Fibrin acts not only to wall off the inflammation, but also permits, via the polymerization of fibrinogen to fibrin, the mechanical trapping of huge numbers of bacteria. This trapping probably represents a very primitive host defense mechanism against microbial invasion. For example, if large numbers of bacteria were permitted free access to the diaphragmatic lymphatics, a lethal septicemia would almost certainly follow. Fibrinous exudates impair the operation of that mechanism. At the same time, however, fibrin isolates the bacteria from the phagocytic host defenses. As few as 100 *E. coli* in a intraperitoneal fibrin clot, will always lead to abscess formation.[27]

BACTERIOLOGY

The Gastrointestinal Flora

The normal empty stomach is sterile because of the germicidal action of free hydrochloric acid, but food and human blood neutralize the acid and bacteria are able to survive. After a meal, bacteria such as Enterobacteriaceae, *Bacteroides,* and lactobacilli from food and saliva reach a concentration of $10^{1.5}$ per ml of gastrointestinal contents.[28] As the stomach empties and the pH again drops below 3, sterility returns (Table 1).

In the normal upper jejunum, the only bacteria regularly found are lactobacilli ($10^{2.4}$ to $10^{4.2}$ bacteria/ml). The proximal ileum and the jejunum have limited flora. The flora of the more distal ileum is rich, however, and its bacterial population is similar in composition to the colon; the distal ileum contains Enterobacteriaceae, *Bacteroides,* and the streptococci, as well as gram-positive nonspore-forming anaerobes. In the left colon, these organisms are found in

TABLE 1. NORMAL INTESTINAL FLORA IN HUMANS (LOG^{10} BACTERIA/ML OF GASTROINTESTINAL CONTENTS).*

	Entero-bacteri-aceae	Bactero-ides	Strepto-cocci	Lacto-bacilli	Gram-positive nonspore-forming anaerobes
Stomach, empty	0	0	0	0	0
Gallbladder	0	0	0	0	0
Stomach, after meal	1.5	1.5	0	1.5	0
Jejunum	<1	<1	2.4-4.2	2.4†	<1
Proximal ileum	<1	0	0	<1	<1
Distal ileum	3.3−5.6	5.2−5.7	2.5−4.9	4.2†	2.5−5.7
Cecum	6.2	7.9	2.6	<1	5.2
Distal colon	6.0−7.6	8.5−10.0	4.0−7.0	3.6−6.4	5.6−10.5

*Adapted from Draser BS, Hill MJ.[28]
†Highly variable.

concentrations that range from 10^4 to 10^{10} bacteria/g of feces. Fungi (usually *Candida albicans*) are present in the bowel contents of most adults.

In pathologic conditions, the bacterial flora in the intestinal tract changes. The stomach of patients with achlorhydria or of those receiving antacids contains Enterobacteriaceae and streptococci. Abnormalities of the small bowel itself (e.g., ileal strictures, diverticulosis, regional enteritis, or fistulas) result in heavy bacterial colonization of the jejunum. Perhaps these alterations also occur in the intestinal tract during nasogastric or intestinal intubation for intestinal obstruction. Obviously, the intestinal flora determines the bacterial population in the initial peritoneal contamination. In one study, no bacteria could be cultured when the normal human duodenum was perforated.[29] When the stomach was perforated, however, cultures were positive for aerobes and anaerobes in 50% and 20%, respectively, of the patients studied. After perforation of the small bowel, 30% of the patients had positive aerobic culture results and 10% were positive for anaerobes. Perforation of the colon or rectum always yielded both aerobes and anaerobes.[29] Purely suppurative lesions usually involve aerobes. In patients with gangrenous infections, aerobes can be cultured from 90% of the patients and anaerobes from 60%.

Familiarity with normal intestinal flora provides only an estimate of the bacterial populations that can be expected in a pathologic situation. In addition to information about pre-existing local flora, it is also important, prior to antibiotic therapy, to know the cause of perforation and the length of time between perforation and the taking of specimens for culture.

In early bacteriologic studies of secondary peritonitis with perforating appendicitis, *E. coli* was found in 80% of all infections and enterococci in 30%.[30] Staphylococci, streptococci, Enterobacteriaceae, *Proteus,* and *Pseudomonas* were isolated less often. *Bacteroides* were cultured in 99% of all isolates and anaerobic streptococci and staphylococci in 88%. Clostridia were detected in only 13% of patients with perforating appendicitis (Table 2).

Adjuvant Substances in the Pathogenesis of Peritonitis

The primary causative agents of peritonitis are bacteria. However, certain substances (adjuvants) augment the effects of bacterial

TABLE 2. BACTERIOLOGY IN THREE
COMBINED STUDIES IN PATIENTS WITH
SECONDARY PERITONITIS.[30,31,39]

	No.	%
Aerobic bacteria		
E. coli	235	60
Streptococcus	108	28
Enterococcus	66	17
Staphylococcus	29	7
Enterobacter/Klebsiella	101	26
Proteus	87	22
Pseudomonas	30	8
Candida	6	2
Anaerobic bacteria		
Bacteroides	288	72
B. fragilis	153	38
Eubacterium	94	24
Clostridium	67	17
Peptostreptococcus	55	14
Peptococcus	42	11
Propionibacterium	36	9
Fusobacterium	34	8

contamination of the peritoneum. Pure suspensions of bacteria alone will not induce peritonitis in animals. Bacteria in combination with foreign substances such as necrotic tissue, sterile feces, barium sulfate, gastric mucin, bile, and hemoglobin will, however, cause peritonitis.[10] Even though the mechanism by which such materials either foster bacterial growth or impair host defenses is unknown, animal research supports the need to evacuate these adjuvants following peritoneal operations.

Bacteriologic Synergism

Other bacteria are probably the most important of all the adjuvants. The colon may contain 10^{10} bacteria/g of feces, with as many as 400 species being present. Very few of these species are found in cases of peritonitis. Competition among the different organisms within the peritoneal cavity and the various degrees of resistance of each species to host defenses leads to restricted growth of many organisms and survival of the most "pathogenic" species.

Using pooled rat fecal contents mixed with barium and implanted in the peritoneal cavities of rats, Onderdonk et al.[35] could identify more than 23 species of bacteria in the fecal implants. The peritoneal cultures however only yielded *E. coli,* enterococci, *Bacteroides,* and *Fusobacterium.* The number of species of bacteria in the original isolate were dramatically reduced. This simplification of the intestinal organisms parallels experience in human intraperitoneal abscesses.[29,36-39] The high initial mortality of the rats was associated with the recovery of *E. coli* in blood cultures. Also, all the surviving animals developed indolent abscesses yielding *B. fragilis* 10^9/ml, *Fusobacterium* 10^9/ml, *E. coli* 10^8/ml, and enterococcus 10^6/ml. In synergy studies, these same investigators[40] determined that no single one of these organisms could produce infection in pure culture in the peritonea cavity but that a mixture of an anaerobe and a facultative aerobe consistently produced intraperitoneal abscesses. Although the experimental model of fecal peritonitis in which *E. coli* and *B. fragilis* predominate is commonly called a biphasic model, it is a prototype of concurrent synergistic infection by two co-pathogens.

There are at least three mechanisms that probably contribute to bacterial synergy: (a) the production by one organism of a nutritional growth factor for the other; (b) the release of a substance(s) that protects against phagocytosis, and (c) the creation of an anaerobic environment.[41] Coliforms, which are known to lower redox potential, would encourage the growth of anaerobes, particularly *Bacteroides.* In addition, *B. fragilis* is capable of inhibiting the phagocytosis of *Proteus mirabilis* in vitro. While antibiotics that kill one organism of a synergistic pair might prevent the growth of another (if administered early enough and in the appropriate concentrations), there is no assurance that killing one organism will indeed eliminate the other. For instance, most *E. coli* are sensitive to gentamicin. While preventing the development of an *E. coli-Bacteroides* abscess, gentamicin can sometimes potentiate a *Bacteroides* infection (without *E. coli*).[43] Furthermore, some bacteria may inactivate antibiotics to which the predominant pathogen is sensitive (e.g., co-infections of a penicillinase-producing organism with a penicillin-sensitive organism, whereby the first protects the pencillin-sensitive bacteria). Certain anaerobic organisms inactivate chloramphenicol, a drug to which both anaerobes and facultative aerobes are sensitive.[44] The best way to treat polymicrobial infections is to treat each pathogen as if it existed in a pure culture.

TREATMENT OF SECONDARY
BACTERIAL PERITONITIS

Preoperative Treatment

Patients with intraperitoneal infection are critically ill. Their treatment should follow certain necessary guidelines for therapy including repeated clinical evaluation and constant monitoring: repeated determinations of blood pressure, pulse, central venous pressure, urine output and specific gravity; laboratory determinations of hematocrit, peripheral leukocyte count, serum electrolytes and serum creatinine; and assessment of the respiratory function by arterial blood gases.

Intraarterial cannulation allows continuous monitoring of the intraarterial blood pressure; and serves as a convenient source of arterial blood for the frequent determination of blood gases and other values.

Loss of fluid volume into the peritoneal cavity results in hypovolemia, which is characteristic of patients with peritonitis. Corrective measures—including plasma fractions, crystalloids, and blood—should be instituted.[46] Maintaining a urinary output of at least 30 ml/hr assures adequate tissue perfusion.

Hypoxemia is common in patients with peritonitis because of the upward diaphragmatic displacement and reflex abdominal rigidity. Respiratory assistance may be required for some patients.

Ileus commonly occurs in peritonitis. Since a reduction in intraluminal pressure might help avoid the breakdown of anastomoses and augment venous return, intestinal intubation may be indicated. This procedure may have a beneficial effect on postoperative recovery and intestinal motility.

Intravenous Feeding

Patients with intraabdominal infections such as peritonitis have metabolic and endocrine demands similar to patients with thermal burns. Their resting metabolic rate can be 40% above the expected value.[47] This deficit may not be reversed with a calorie intake as high as 3,000 to 4,000 calories/day. Unlike individuals undergoing elective operations, patients with peritonitis act as if they are in a protracted traumatic state.

Patients with intraabdominal infections have elevated circulating glucocorticoid, catecholamine, insulin, and glucagon levels. These and other neurohumoral responses cause these patients to become insulin-resistant. Their primary source of energy is protein that can be mobilized from the peripheral muscle. Because protein is a relatively inefficient source of calories, infusions of amino acids along with other caloric preparations are the most efficient means of sparing muscle-wasting in massively catabolic patients.[48] Hyperalimentation via a central venous catheter may be necessary.[49] Usually, infusions containing 1 calorie/ml are used, totaling 3,000 to 4,000 calories/day.

Antibiotics

Antibiotic therapy is begun as soon as peritoneal infection is diagnosed even before samples of peritoneal fluid can be taken for Gram staining and for aerobic and anaerobic cultures. Although the initial antibiotic therapy is given on a presumptive or an empiric basis, the antibacterials selected should be rational. The agents should be active against the suspected offending organisms and should achieve inhibitory concentrations in the peritoneal exudate. Fortunately, most antibiotics reach therapeutic levels in the intraperitoneal fluid.[50,51]

Perforation of the upper gastrointestinal tract results in infection with predominantly gram-positive organisms. Delays in treatment enable gram-negative facultative aerobes to overgrow in combination with gram-positive anaerobes; this is a potentially synergistic combination. In patients with mid to lower intestinal perforations, those antibiotics that eradicate the coliforms, the enterococci, and the anaerobic organisms, especially B. fragilis, should be chosen. The usual antibiotic sensitivities of these organisms are known, and the combination of an aminoglycoside with ampicillin and clindamycin has the required spectrum of activity and is the "gold standard" against which all other antibiotic regimens should be compared.

It is important to eradicate all of the bacterial co-pathogens as early as possible to prevent the development of abscesses and delayed sepsis. It is irrational and potentially dangerous to await the outgrowth of a predominant pathogen prior to instituting antibacterial therapy. Clinical manifestations of sepsis and abscess formation that result from the overgrowth of the two predominant pathogens of peritonitis, E. coli and B. fragilis, respectively, may not be simultaneous; however, the implantation of these organisms following perforation are simultaneous events. For this reason, infections caused by *E. coli* and *B. fragilis* should be treated early and aggressively to eliminate septic complications and to prevent abscess formation.

The vast majority of strains of *E. coli, Klebsiella, Enterobacter,* and *Proteus* are sensitive to the aminoglycosides. Although, *Pseudomonas* is of concern in seriously ill hospitalized patients because of its presence in the hospital flora and its variable antibiotic sensitivity, *Pseudomonas* is rarely a problem in peritonitis. As a rule, peak blood levels of gentamicin or tobramycin should not exceed 12 mcg/ml or fall below 6 mcg/ml. Trough levels should always be less than 2 mcg/ml. Such a therapeutic range limits toxicity and provides efficacy at high and low concentrations, respectively. In patients with impaired renal function, the dosage should be reduced appropriately. In all cases, aminoglycoside blood levels must be monitored. There is no convincing evidence which favors the use of one aminoglycoside over another.

B. fragilis is a common organism in intraabdominal infections, but anaerobes are not susceptible to the aminoglycosides, in fact evidence suggests aminoglycoside therapy alone can selectively foster the growth of *B. fragilis*.[52] Antibiotics effective against *B. fragilis* should be used in combination with an aminoglycoside for such infections. Clindamycin and metronidazole are both effective against essentially all anaerobes and strains of *Bacteroides.*

Most investigators[38] now agree that *B. fragilis* is an important co-pathogen especially in the pathogenesis of abscesses. Weinstein et al.[54] evaluated the ability of anaerobes to cause abscess formation. Using a standardized inoculum of feces in rats and specific antimicrobial probes—clindamycin for anaerobes and gentamicin for gram-negative aerobes, they were able to demonstrate the role of aerobes and anaerobes in peritonitis. The untreated rats had a two-stage disease: Initially, acute peritonitis was associated with a 37% mortality; all surviving rats developed indolent intraabdominal abscesses. Although treatment with gentamicin reduced the acute mortality to 4%, 98% of the surviving animals developed abscesses. The use of clindamycin alone was associated with 35% mortality, but the incidence of intraabdominal abscesses was only 5%. A combination of gentamicin plus clindamycin resulted in a 7% mortality, with a 6% incidence of abscess formation.

Clindamycin can cause diarrhea and pseudomembranous colitis.[55] Many other antibiotics have been shown to be associated with diarrhea caused by a toxin produced by *Clostridium difficile*. The *C. difficile* colitis is less likely to develop if therapy is discontinued at the first sign of diarrhea. Metronidazole is effective against most strains of *C. difficile* and one would expect that metronidazole would be associated with fewer cases of antibiotic associated colitis. Bartlett, in an extensive experience, has seen only one case associated with metronidazole. Vancomycin is effective against antibiotic-associated colitis produced by *C. difficile*. The usual adult dosage of vanomycin is 500 mg orally every six hours for seven to ten days.

Enterococci have been found to be "breakthrough" organisms in patients with sepsis caused by enteric polymicrobial flora treated with an aminoglycoside and clindamycin.[52,57] Thus, we recommend that ampicillin be used to treat enterococci found in the peritoneal cavity after viscus perforation. Even though this organism is rarely pathogenic by itself, it is probably an important co-pathogen. The triple antibiotic regimen is the standard against which other antibiotics should be compared. Several newer antibiotics are good second choices. Cefoxitin is a newer cephalosporin derivative with an expanded spectrum encompassing many *B. fragilis* strains. The third generation cephalosporins (moxalactam, cefotaxime, cefaperazone, etc.) have a broader spectrum against gram-negative bacilli and *B. fragilis*. To date, no published studies have shown that the use of these antibiotics as sole agents in peritonitis are better than the combination of an aminoglycoside and clindamycin. The high incidence of infection caused by resistant gram-negative aerobes may preclude the use of cefoxitin alone for the treatment of intraabdominal sepsis.[58] Cefoxitin is effective as a substitute for clindamycin but *C. difficile* colitis has also been reported after cefoxitin treatment.

Metronidazole is probably the equivalent of clindamycin in combination with an aminoglycoside. Chloramphenicol acts against both gram-negative and gram-positive aerobic and anaerobic pathogens associated with gastrointestinal perforation (including enterococci and *Bacteroides*). Chloramphenicol does not require dosage adjustments when renal malfunction occurs and is the accepted antibiotic for patients with peritonitis and renal failure. There have been recent reports, however, of clinical failure with chloramphenicol in patients with intraabdominal sepsis. This failure may be explained by the fact that chloramphenicol can be inactivated by some anaerobes.[44,59] Chloramphenicol alone may not be considered an ideal drug in mixed intra-peritoneal infections, although it is a good alternative choice.

Operation

Although nonoperative therapy is the treatment of choice in primary peritonitis, the goal of an operation in peritonitis is to eliminate the continuing source of peritoneal contamination and to prevent abscess formation.

There are two schools of thought concerning the operative management of the peritoneal cavity.[1] The more traditional method is dependent upon the natural tendency of the peritoneal cavity to loculate infected material and form abscesses. This method requires the smallest possible incision necessary to expose and then to seal the perforation; the peritoneal cavity is not irrigated. Drains are placed into abscess pockets and no attempt is made to debride the abscess wall. This technique is effective when the peritonitis is relatively well localized especially when the disease is adjacent to the abdominal wall.[2]

In the other approach, a generous incision is made, all spaces and potential spaces are evacuated, and the entire peritoneal cavity is washed free of all adjuvant substances (e.g., gastric mucin, bile, blood, or necrotic tissue), and free circulation is established within the peritoneal cavity to facilitate the normal mechanisms of lymphatic bacterial clearance.[2,60]

Hudspeth[61] believes that complete exposure of the peritoneal cavity is necessary for adequate operative debridement; complete irrigation with saline is then instituted until the effluent is clear. Debridement, irrigation, and cleansing are continued until the peritoneum is grossly free of fibrin. Although Hudspeth[61] does not use local antibiotics, other evidence supports their use.[62-66] Hudspeth labelled his procedure "radical peritoneal debridement." Although the approach is rational, many surgeons are uncertain how "radical" to be. The danger is that the procedure will be so traumatic that more fibrin will be laid down and bleeding will be initiated. The purpose of the debridement will then be compromised by the outpouring of more adjuvant substances (fibrin, hemoglobin).

Many surgeons have performed investigations of some of the operative approaches in experimental models. Most studies fail to show either a beneficial or a detrimental effect of saline irrigation on the contaminated peritoneal cavity of experimental animals.[64,67] Saline is probably ineffective in removing the bacteria trapped in fibrin. In addition, we[68] have clearly shown the detrimental effects of leaving saline in the contaminated peritoneal cavity. Saline apparently dilutes the bacterial opsonins so that bacterial phagocytosis cannot take place. When saline irrigation is used in patients to remove bacteria and necrotic debris, all the excess fluid should be aspirated before closure. For this reason, continuous saline irrigation of the peritoneal cavity with saline via indwelling intraperitoneal catheters seems inadvisable. Not only will the phagocytes be diluted and rendered nonfunctional and the opsonins diluted, but the antibiotic concentrations in the peritoneal cavity will be reduced. If continuous peritoneal irrigation is used, antimicrobials should probably be added to the irrigant.

Although there is concern that intraoperative peritoneal irrigation can contribute to generalized contamination, there is no evidence that spread is harmful in patients with adequate blood levels of antibiotics. Many surgeons hope to minimize the contamination by using antibiotics in the irrigating solution. It is generally accepted that local application of antibiotics in experimental peritonitis can lower mortality significantly.[64,65] Clinical studies have yielded conflicting results. While no studies have demonstrated harmful effects from local irrigation with antibiotics at the time of operation, some have shown a reduction in intraperitoneal abscess formation,[69] and others have shown no benefit.[70]

Topical antibiotics are probably redundant in most cases of generalized peritonitis because most systemic antibiotics reach the normal peritoneal cavity in concentrations that will inhibit bacteria in vitro.[51] The penetration capability of antibiotics into infected peritoneal loculations, however, is unknown. So far the reports indicate that antibiotic penetration into artificially created, fibrous-lined, infected cavities is poor.

The bulk of clinical and experimental evidence supports the local application of antibiotics and irrigation of the peritoneal cavity during an operation as valuable adjuncts for the treatment of disseminated peritoneal infections. We use a 0.1% solution of cephalothin to irrigate the contaminated peritoneal cavity throughout the operation. This dose is approved by the FDA for this purpose. Such a high, local concentration extends the antibacterial spectrum to almost all enteric flora including B. fragilis. In addition, most of our patients with peritonitis are treated with a combination of systemic ampicillin, an aminoglycoside, and clindamycin. A topical aminoglycoside (especially neomycin) should not be used because there is a risk of respiratory, renal, and auditory complications.

If topical intraoperative cephalosporins are used, it is important to prolong contact between bacteria and irrigant because these agents do not kill on contact. They therefore cannot be expected to be effective, if their use is restricted to a final rinse. The use of continuous postoperative intraperitoneal antibiotic infusions is even more controversial. Repeated intraperitoneal antibiotic infusions have been shown to reduce the incidence of intraperitoneal infections in patients with perforating appendicitis.[69,71]

A number of investigators have reduced the mortality and the incidence of late intraperitoneal abscess formation by using continuous postoperative peritoneal lavage via indwelling catheters.[72,74] Continuous peritoneal lavage, with large volumes of fluid containing antibiotics, has the theoretical advantages of a complete washing action, which may also minimize loculations. The potential disadvantage is that the opsonins are diluted so that phagocytes cannot operate effectively in such a fluid medium. In addition, the concentration of intraperitoneal antibiotics will be reduced unless the irrigant contains additional amounts.

Drainage

Drainage of the peritoneal cavity will be ineffective unless peritoneal lavage is used because the drains are rapidly walled off by fibrin deposition along the tract.[75,76] Walled-off abscesses, the damaged pancreas plus pancreatic, biliary, or intestinal fistulas should always be drained. Otherwise drains are ineffective at best and may be dangerous because bacteria pass along them into the peritoneal cavity.

Prevention of Intraperitoneal Abscesses after Peritonitis

Abscesses evolve continuously as a result of the body's incomplete attempt to localize and destroy insoluble toxic substances or organisms. The exact processes of formation are poorly understood. Bacterial invasion causes the activation of complement and tissue injury to release vasoactive substances and chemotactic factors. Increased capillary permeability leads to edema and release of neutrophils that phagocytose opsonized bacteria (Figure 5). Fibrinous adhesions form between the serosal surfaces and fibrin is formed in the surrounding interstitial tissues.

Thrombosis of capillaries and venules within the edematous and necrotic tissue is apparently manifested only in severe tissue injury. Even the lymphatic vessels normally remain patent, because they are held open by anchoring filaments despite the presence of edema.[77] Small bacterial insults, therefore, can be well tolerated but severe or continuous bacterial contamination that is uncontrolled by opsonins and phagocytes or not aspirated into the diaphragmatic lymphatics will form abscesses in a delicate balance with the local host defenses.

Even under normal circumstances, neutrophils in tissue have a self-limited life span of three to five days.[7] In individuals who do not have an infection, approximately 100 g of neutrophils die every day. When a neutrophil leaves the vascular compartment, it will never return to the circulation. Abscess formation depends on the development of an avascular, fibrinous—and later, fibrous—wall and on the release of lysosomal enzymes from the dead and dying neutrophils within.

Lysosomes contain enzymes—including collagenases, elastinases, proteinases, and fibrinolysin activators—that can degrade all classes of macromolecules.[78] Little is known about the effect of these enzymes on the solubility, absorption, or toxic properties of bacterial endotoxins. The breakdown products are osmotically active. These breakdown products are therefore responsible for the tendency of abscesses to increase in size and dissect through new tissue planes. Intraperitoneal abscesses can resolve spontaneously although they can rupture into blood vessels to cause septicemia or into serous cavities (such as pleura, pericardium, or peritoneum). They may also rupture into adjacent viscera, which may result in fistula formation or through the surgical incision, or even through the intact abdominal wall.

Foreign bodies are sometimes responsible for the persistence of an infection as well as for abscess formation. To produce an intradermal abscess experimentally, 10^6 *Staphylococcus aureus* are required. The presence of a single silk suture[79] reduces the number of organisms required to produce infection to 10^2. Obviously, feces or other retained foreign material (e.g., drains) are especially prone to augment the formation of abscesses.

The normal defense mechanisms tend to form the development of abscesses by the very same mechanism by which septicemia from peritonitis is avoided. Fibrin is a very effective bacterial trap—but trapped bacteria are isolated from the phagocytes which penetrate fibrin slowly. If peritoneal fibrinolysis is inhibited, as it is during peritonitis, the fibrin clots tend to persist and abscesses occur. For this reason, debridement of fibrino-purulent debris should probably be carried out at the initial operation. The abscessogenic effects of contaminated fibrin is proportional to its volume so that stripping wisps of fibrin off the serosol surface is probably not indicated.

The penetration of antibiotics—and possibly of other components such as complement and serum opsonins—into cavities and fibrin clots is poor:[80] the inflammatory sealing around the abscess may be too efficient, which explains why the nonoperative treatment of mature abscesses is often unsuccessful. On the other hand, when the abscess is immature (with patent capillaries and lymphatics within the fibrinous walls), antibiotic therapy alone without drainage can sometimes be effective. The early use of effective antibiotics, administered as close to the time of the insult as possible, may therefore prevent abscess formation.

Certain bacteria appear to be "abscessogenic." For example, staphylococci secrete tissue-destructive enzymes and coagulases that promote local rather than distant sepsis. Anaerobic organisms need the low redox potential that is associated with necrotic and avascular tissue. The peritoneal cavity itself becomes analogous to the cavity of an abscess after the serous membranes have been separated by fluid exudates. With long distances to be transversed to the nearest capillaries, the intraperitoneal oxygen tension is significantly lowered.[81] Both anaerobes and the facultative bacteria, which also grow well under anaerobic conditions, therefore, can be found in intraperitoneal abscesses.

The bacterial population associated with intraperitoneal abscesses is usually simpler than that of free peritonitis. Free peritonitis from fecal contents of rats consists of numerous species of organisms that can grow in the culture-like medium of the peritoneal cavity.[82] Experimentally, the number of microbial species is reduced in rats that survive to develop abscesses. Nevertheless, most of these abscesses remain polymicrobial and probably represent synergistic infections. The bacteria most commonly associated with experimental abscesses after fecal contamination of the peritoneal cavity of rats are *E. coli,* enterococci (facultative aerobes), *B. fragilis,* and *Fusobacterium* (obligate anaerobes).[40]

In the animal model, any combination of a facultative aerobe with an anaerobe will cause the formation of abscesses. In humans, intraabdominal abscesses sometimes yield a single species of bacteria. However, when careful anaerobic culturing methods are used, the incidence of such a finding is reduced.[32,83]

Abscess formation is one of the natural responses to peritoneal contamination, therefore, studies on peritonitis often overlap with studies on intraperitoneal abscesses. As can be seen from Figure 5, the two diseases obviously represent an evolving condition.

A case of diffuse peritonitis with multiple pockets of loculated fluid may represent multiple early abscesses. When a condition is labelled "peritonitis," it may be treated differently than if called an "abscess" which might be drained externally.

Residual abscess formation should be uncommon when the source of peritoneal contamination is eliminated; foreign bodies are excluded from the peritoneal cavity (this includes removal of all blood, mucin, feces, and bile); the bacteria are washed out or killed with local antibiotics; all fibrinous barriers to the free circulation of fluid within the peritoneal cavity are eliminated; foreign bodies are excluded from the peritoneal activity (this includes removal of all blood, mucin, feces, and bile); the bacteria are washed out or killed with local antibiotics; all fibrinous barriers to the free circulation of fluid within the peritoneal cavity are eliminated; diaphragmatic motion is unimpaired; and host phagocytic defenses are adequate. In short, the proper operative management of peritonitis should minimize the risk of residual abscess formation.

Intraperitoneal bacterial abscesses sometimes result from a slowly developing perforation of a viscus (e.g., appendix, gallbladder, or colon), prior operation on the gastrointestinal tract (e.g., an anastomotic leak), or an incompletely managed peritonitis. If untreated, abscesses can cause lethal sepsis. Unfortunately they are difficult to detect, and many surgeons delay diagnostic or treatment procedures until the presence of an abscess is fully confirmed. Available diagnostic techniques are primarily designed to locate a known abscess rather than to diagnose its existence. Any delay can be fatal, so it is important to initiate therapy as soon as there is a suspicion that such an abscess does exist.

REFERENCES

1. Steinberg B: Infections of the Peritoneum. New York, Paul Hoeber, Inc., 1944.
2. Hau T, Ahrenholz DH, and Simmons RL: Secondary bacterial peritonitis: The biologic basis of treatment. Cur Prob Surg 16:No. 10, 1979.
3. Ahrenholz DH, Simmons RL: Peritonitis and other intraabdominal infections. Chapter 34 in Surgical Infectious Diseases, R.L. Simmons, R.J. Howard (eds), Appleton-Century-Crofts, 1982, p. 795.
4. Maddox JR, et al.: Appendectomies in a children's hospital: A five-year study. Arch Surg 89:223, 1964.
5. Bolman RMH, et al.: Perforated appendicitis: 391 cases without mortality. Arch Surg 74:719, 1957.
6. Allen L: The peritoneal stomata. Anat Rec 67:89, 1936.
7. Egdahl RH: Current mortality in appendicity. Am J Surg 107:757, 1964.
8. Ariel IM, Kazarian KK (eds): Diagnosis and Treatment of Abdominal Abscesses. Baltimore, Williams & Wilkins, 1971.
9. Miller DW, Wichern WA Jr: Perforated sigmoid diverticulitis: Appraisal of primary versus delayed resection. Am J Surg 121:536, 1971.

10. Welch JP, Donaldson GA: Perforative carcinoma of colon and rectum. Ann Surg 180:734, 1974.
11. Dawson JL: A study of some factors affecting the mortality rate in diffuse peritonitis. Gut 4:368, 1963.
12. Braun L, et al.: Die fortgeschrittene diffuse peritonitis. Bruns' Beitrage zur Klinschen Chirurgie 221:120, 1974.
13. Henderson LW: The problem of peritoneal membrane area and permeability. Kidney Int 3:409, 1973.
14. Costain WA: Lymphaticostomy in peritonitis. Surg Gynecol Obstet 36:365, 1923.
15. Fowler GR: Diffuse septic peritonitis, with special reference to a new method of treatment, namely, the elevated head and trunk posture, to facilitate drainage into the pelvis: With a report of nine consecutive cases of recovery. Med Rec 57:617, 1900.
16. Courtice FC, et al.: The removal of free red blood cells from the peritoneal cavity of animals. Aust J Exp Biol Med Sci 31:215, 1953.
17. Autio V: The spread of intraperitoneal infection. Acta Chir Scand (Suppl) 321, 1964.
18. Ryan GB, et al.: Mesothelial injury and recovery. Am J Pathol 71:93, 1973.
19. Buckman RF Jr, et al.: A unifying pathogenic mechanism in the etiology of intraperitoneal adhesions. J Surg Res 20:1, 1976.
20. Hau T, Payne WD, Simmons RL: Fibrinolytic activity of the peritoneum during experimental peritonitis. Surgery Gynecol Obstet 148:415–418, 1979.
21. Ryan GB, et al.: Postoperative peritoneal adhesions: A study of the mechanisms. Am J Pathol 65:117, 1971.
22. Benzer Von H, et al.: Uber zusammenhange zwischen fibrinolyse und intraperitonealen adhasionen. Wien Klin Wochenschr 75:881, 1963.
23. Hau T, Simmons RL: Heparin in the treatment of experimental peritonitis. Ann Surg 187:294, 1978
24. Ellis H: The cause and prevention of postoperative intraperitoneal adhesions. Surg Gynecol Obstet 133:497, 1971.
25. Hau T, Lee JT, Simmons RL: Mechanisms of the adjuvant effect of hemoglobin in experimental peritonitis: I. In vivo inhibition of peritoneal leucocytosis. Surgery 83:223, 1978.
26. Landman MD, Longmire, WP Jr: Neural and hormonal influences of peritonitis on paralytic ileus. Am Surg 33:756, 1967.
27. Ahrenholz DH, Simmons RL: Fibrin in peritonitis: I. Beneficial and adverse effects of fibrin in experimental E. coli peritonitis. Surgery 88:41–47, 1980.
28. Draser BS, Hill MJ: Human Intestinal Flora. London, Academic Press, 1974.
29. Stone HH, et al.: Incidence and significance of intraperitoneal anaerobic bacteria. Ann Surg 181:705, 1975.
30. Altemeier WA: The bacterial flora of acute perforated appendicitis with

24   R.L. SIMMONS AND D.H. AHRENHOLZ

peritonitis: A bacteriologic study based upon one hundred cases. Ann Surg 107:517, 1938.
31. Gorbach SL, et al.: Anaerobic microorganisms in intraabdominal infections, in Balows A, et al. (eds): Anaerobic Bacteria: Role in Disease. Springfield, Ill, Charles C. Thomas Publisher, 1974, p. 399.
32. Lorber B, Swenson RM: The bacteriology of intraabdominal infections. Surg Clin North Am 55:1349, 1975.
33. Florey H: Reactions of, and absorption by, lymphatics, with special reference to those of the diaphragm. Br J Exp Pathol 8:479, 1927.
34. Dixon, CF, Rixford, EL: Cytologic response to peritoneal irrigation in man: A protective mechanism. Am J Surg 25:504, 1934.
35. Onderdonk A, et al.: Experimental intraabdominal abscesses in rats: Quantitative bacteriology of infected animals. Infect Immun 10:1256, 1974.
36. Artz CP, et al.: Further studies concerning the pathogenesis and treatment of peritonitis. Ann Surg 155:756, 1962.
37. Meleney F, et al.: Peritonitis: I. The correlation of the bacteriology of the peritoneal exudates and the clinical course of the disease in 106 cases of peritonitis. Arch Surg 22:1, 1931.
38. Thadepalli H, et al.: Abdominal trauma, anaerobes, and antibiotics. Surg Gynecol Obstet 137:27, 1973.
39. Altemeier WA, et al.: Intraabdominal abscesses. Am J Surg 125:70, 1973.
40. Onderdonk A, et al.: Microbial surgery in experimental intraabdominal abscesses. Infect Immun 13:22, 1976.
41. Mackowiak PA: Microbial synergism in human infections (2 parts). N Engl J Med 298:21, 83, 1978.
42. Hagen JC, et al.: Interaction of *Bacteroides fragilis* and *Escherichia coli* in intraperitoneal abscess formation. Abstract 450, 16th Interscience Conference on Antimicrobial Agents and Chemotherapy. Chicago, October 17–29, 1976.
43. Rotilie-Quinter CA, et al.: Gentamicin potentiation of *Bacteroides fragilis* infection. Abstract 173, 17th Interscience Conference on Antimicrobial Agents and Chemotherapy, New York, October 12–14, 1977.
44. Louie TJ, et al.: Failure of chloramphenicol therapy of experimental intraabdominal sepsis. Abstract 25, 17th Interscience Conference on Antimicrobial Agents and Chemotherapy. New York, October 12–14, 1977.
45. Ohlsson K: Collagenase and elastase released during peritonitis are complexed by plasma protease inhibitors. Surgery 79:652, 1976.
46. Moore FD: Metabolic care of the surgical patient. Philadelphia, W.B. Saunders Co, 1959.
47. Kinney JM: The effect of injury on metabolism. Br J Surg 54:435, 1967.
48. Miller JDB, et al.: Effect of deep surgical sepsis on protein-sparing therapies and nitrogen balance. Am J Clin Nutr 30:1528, 1977.

49. Dudrick SJ, Rhoades JE: Metabolism in surgical patients: Protein, carbohydrate and fat utilization by oral and parenteral routes, in Sabiston D (ed): Davis-Christopher Textbook of Surgery. Philadelphia, W.B. Saunders Co, 1977, p. 150.
50. Gerding DN, Hall WH: The penetration of antibiotics into peritoneal fluid. Bull NY Acad Med 51:1016, 1975.
51. Gerding DN, et al.: Antibiotic concentrations in ascitic fluid of patients with ascites and bacterial peritonitis. Ann Intern Med 86:708, 1977.
52. Fass RJ: Treatment of mixed bacterial infections with clindamycin and gentamicin. J Infect Dis 135:S74, 1977.
53. Sen P, et al.: Prospective evaluation of combinations of antimicrobial agents for endometritis after cesarean section. Surg Gynecol Obstet 151:89, 1980.
54. Weinstein WM, et al.: Antimicrobial therapy of experimental intraabdominal sepsis. J Infect Dis 132:282, 1975.
55. Tedesco FJ: Clindamycin and colitis: A review. J Infect Dis 135:S95, 1977.
56. Bartlett JG, et al.: Empiric treatment with clindamycin and gentamicin of suspected sepsis due to anaerobic and aerobic bacteria. J Infect Dis 135:S80, 1977.
57. Ledger WJ, et al.: Bacteremia on an obstetric-gynecologic service. Am J Obstet Gynecol 121:205, 1975.
58. Mulligan ME: Contamination of a hospital environment by Clostridium difficile. Curr Microbiol 3:173–175, 1979.
59. Thadepalli H, et al.: Apparent failure of chloramphenicol in the treatment of anaerobic infections. Curr Ther Res 22:421, 1977.
60. Dunphy JE: Peritoneal cavity, in Dunphy JE, Way LW (eds): Current Surgical Diagnosis and Treatment. Los Altos, Calif, Lange Medical Publications, 1977, p. 25.
61. Hudspth AS: Radical surgery debridement in the treatment of advanced generalized bacterial peritonitis. Arch Surg 110:1233, 1975.
62. DiVincenti FC, Cohn I Jr: Intraperitoneal kanamycin in advanced peritonitis: A preliminary report. Surgery 55:841, 1964.
63. Noon GP, et al.: Clinical evaluation of peritoneal irrigation with antibiotic solution. Surgery 62:73, 1967.
64. Schumer W, et al.: Peritoneal lavage in postoperative therapy of late peritoneal sepsis: Preliminary report. Surgery 55:841, 1964.
65. Sleeman HK, et al.: Value of antibiotics, corticosteroids, and peritoneal lavage in the treatment of experimental peritonitis. Surgery 66:1060, 1969.
66. Smith EB: Adjuvant therapy of generalized peritonitis with intraperitoneally administered cephalothin. Surg Gynecol Obstet 136:441, 1973.
67. Rosato EF, et al.: Peritoneal lavage treatment in experimental peritonitis. Ann Surg 175:384, 1972.
68. Ahrenholz DH: Effect of intraperitoneal fluid on mortality of Es-

cherichia coli peritonitis. Surg Forum 30:483–484, 1979.

69. Fowler R: A controlled trial of intraperitoneal cephaloridin administration in peritonitis. J Pediatr Surg 10:43, 1975.

70. Rambo WM: Irrigation of the peritoneal cavity with cephalothin. Am J Surg 123:192, 1972.

71. DiVincenti FC, Cohn I Jr: Prolonged administration of intraperitoneal kanamycin in the treatment of peritonitis. Am Surg 37:177, 1971.

72. Bhushan C, et al.: Continuous postoperative peritoneal lavage in diffuse peritonitis using balanced saline antibiotic solution. Int Surg 60:256, 1975.

73. Hunt JA, et al.: Antibiotic peritoneal lavage in severe peritonitis: A preliminary assessment. S Afr Med J 49:233, 1975.

74. Kiene S, Troeger H: Intraperitoneale antibiotkaspuldrainage bei diffuser peritonitis. Zentralbl Chir 99:833, 1974.

75. Hermann G: Intraperitoneal drainage. Surg Clin North Am 49:1279, 1969.

76. Yates JL: An experimental study of the local effects of peritoneal drainage. Surg Gynecol Obstet 1:473, 1905.

77. Casley-Smith JR: The lymphatic system in inflammation, in Zweifach BW, et al. (eds): The Inflammatory Process, 2nd ed. New York, Academic Press, 1973, vol 2, p. 161.

78. Murphy P: The Neutrophil. New York, Plenum Medical Book Co, 1976.

79. Elek SD, Conen PE: The virulence of *Staphylococcus pyogenes* for man: A study of the problems of wound infection. Br J Exp Pathol 38:573, 1957.

80. Gerding DN, et al.: Cefamandole (CM) and cefazolin (CZ) levels in uninfected peritoneal capsules and *E. coli* capsule abscesses. Abstract 30, 17th Interscience Conference on Antimicrobial Agents and Chemotherapy, New York, October 12–14, 1977.

81. Renvall S, Niinikoski J: Intraperitoneal oxygen and carbon dioxide tensions in experimental adhesion disease and peritonitis. Am J Surg 130:286, 1975.

82. Weinstein WM, et al.: Experimental intraabdominal abscesses in rats: Development of an experimental model. Infect Immunol 10:1250, 1974.

83. Wang SMS, Wilson SE: Subphrenic abscess: The new epidemiology. Arch Surg 112:934, 1977.

CHAPTER TWO

The Role of Anaerobes in Intraabdominal Surgical Infections

Ronald Lee Nichols, M.D.

INTRODUCTION

The incidence of infectious complications following either elective or emergency operations markedly increases if the gastrointestinal tract has been damaged by trauma, disease, or the operation itself. These complications are due, almost solely, to the overwhelming of normal host defense mechanisms in adjacent tissues by escaped endogenous gastrointestinal microflora. Most such infections occur in the operative wound, but less frequently intraabdominal infections result; and these, i.e., peritonitis and abscess, present greater diagnostic and therapeutic problems to the surgeon.

As long ago as 1938, Altemeier[1] stressed the polymicrobial nature of the bacterial flora of peritonitis resulting from acute appendiceal perforation. In 1942, he reported[2] on the pathogenicity of the microorganisms isolated from such patients in experimental animals. Until comparatively recently, very little information was added to Altemeier's findings. However, the application of modern collection, preserving and culturing techniques, and the study of anaerobic bacteria has, in the past six or seven years, demonstrated the important role of obligate anaerobes in intraabdominal infections.[3]

ENDOGENOUS MICROFLORA

Human endogenous microflora is composed of both aerobic and anaerobic organisms. Many of the aerobes are facultative, or capable of growing and multiplying with or without oxygen, while the fastidious anaerobes show optimal growth only in an environment of reduced oxygen tension.

Both aerobes and anaerobes are isolated at all levels of the gastrointestinal tract, with types and predominance of flora varying from mouth to colon (Table 1).[4]

In the oropharynx, the predominant aerobes include Neisseria, Streptococcus, and Hemophilus. The anaerobes, which outnumber aerobes 10:1, include *Bacteroides oralis, B. melaninogenicus,* peptostrepticoccus, and Fusibacterium, a predominance that is increased by poor dental hygiene and periodontal disease.

Each swallow contaminates the esophagus with these oral organisms. In most healthy people, however—or in those with chronic duodenal ulcer—gastric microflora is either minimal or absent, thanks to the inhibitory action of gastric acid and normal gastric motility. Polymicrobial microflora are found in the stomachs of most patients undergoing surgery for gastric ulcer, bleeding or obstructive duodenal ulcer, or gastric carcinoma.[2]

The low concentrations of both aerobes and anaerobes found in the duodenum and proximal small intestine are transient, reaching clinically relevant amounts only in the absence of intestinal obstruction. In disease, the normally sterile biliary tract is found to contain mostly aerobic enteric organisms such as the coliforms and enterococci.

The distal ileum contains significant numbers of both aerobic coliforms and anaerobes, including *B. fragilis.* Finally, the colon harbors the greatest concentration of microflora, reaching 10^{10} to 10^{11} per gram of stool, which is once again 10:1 anaerobic.

SPECIMEN COLLECTION AND
LABORATORY DIAGNOSIS

For optimum recovery of anaerobic organisms from an intraabdominal infection, the specimen should be obtained from deep within the active site of infection. This prevents surface contamination and exposure to atmospheric oxygen. Direct needle aspiration is the best approach, with anaerobic conditions maintained by bending or plugging the needle immediately after collection. The specimen is

TABLE 1. ENDOGENOUS HUMAN MICROFLORA. [4]

Region	Predominant microflora	Concentration (per g or ml of aspirate)		Predominant organisms	
		Aerobes	Anaerobes	Aerobes	Anaerobes
Oropharynx	Slight predominance of anaerobic organisms	10^4 to 10^5	10^5 to 10^7	Streptococcus Hemophilus Neisseria Diptheroids	Peptostreptococcus Fusobacterium *Bacteroides melaninogenicus* *Bacteroides oralis* Peptococcus
Esophagus	Slight anaerobic predominance	10^4 to 10^5	10^5 to 10^7	Streptococcus Hemophilus Neisseria	Peptostreptococcus Fusobacterium *B. melaninogenicus* *B. oralis* Peptococcus
Stomach	Both aerobic and anaerobic (when present)	Microflora is absent or minimal if normal gastric acidity and motility are present.		Streptococcus *Escherichia coli* Klebsiella Enterobacter Enterococcus	Peptostreptococcus *B. oralis* *B. melaninogenicus*

(cont.)

TABLE 1. ENDOGENOUS HUMAN MICROFLORA. (Continued)

Region	Predominant microflora	Concentration (per g or ml of aspirate)		Predominant organisms	
		Aerobes	Anaerobes	Aerobes	Anaerobes
Biliary tract	Great aerobic predominance (when present)	No concentrations in healthy persons		E. coli Klebsiella Enterobacter Enterococcus	Clostridium Bacteroides fragilis
Proximal small intestine	Slight predominance of aerobic organisms	10^2	10 to 10^2	Streptococcus E. coli Klebsiella Enterobacter Enterococcus	Peptostreptococcus B oralis B. melanino-genicus

Distal ileum	Slight predominance of aerobic organisms	10^4 to 10^6	10^5 to 10^7	E. coli Klebsiella Enterobacter Enterococcus	B. fragilis Peptostreptococcus Clostridium
Colon	Great predominance of anaerobic organisms	10^5 to 10^8	10^9 to 10^{11}	E. coli Klebsiella Enterobacter Enterococcus	B. fragilis Peptostreptococcus Clostridium
Vagina	Slight anaerobic predominance	Difficult to accurately quantitate		Lactobacillus E. coli	B. fragilis Peptostreptococcus Clostridium B. melaninogenicus Bifidobacterium

then delivered promptly to the laboratory for Gram's stain and culture.

Gram's stain characteristics and odor—putrid odor strongly suggests anaerobic infection—can often predict culture results. The stain is crucial, in any case, to provide evidence for a presumptive diagnosis (Table 2).[5] It ensures that culture results account for all recognized morphotypes and helps species identification, given the sometimes unique morphologies of anaerobes.

For best culture results, specimens must be inoculated promptly on specialized media with minimum exposure to air. Initially, two media should be inoculated: enriched preparations such as Brucella blood agar with vitamin K and hemin for anaerobic growth and vancomycin and kanamycin to discourage facultative overgrowth; and a tube of chopped meat glucose broth, to assure recovery of all species. At 24 to 48 hours, the broth inoculum is usually plated. Optimum incubation time for the slow-growing anaerobes is 72 to 96 hours.

Although inoculation is preferably, and most easily, done in an anaerobic chamber, the less expensive GasPak (Figure 1) anaerobic jar system permits recovery of most anaerobes.

Identification of anaerobic organisms, which by biochemical fermentation usually takes several days, can be made tentatively within three or four days on the basis of Gram's stain and gas chromatography. Gas chromatography of a pure broth culture produces characteristic patterns which, together with Gram's stain results, usually identify genus and, occasionally, species.

ETIOLOGY AND SITES OF
INTRAABDOMINAL SEPSIS

Perforated appendicitis and diverticulitis are the disease states most commonly associated with intraabdominal sepsis. According to Altmeier and associates, the two conditions were responsible for more than a quarter of 500 intraabdominal infections over 10 years.[6]

Such infections are also associated with perforation of the stomach or duodenum, spontaneous leak from gastrointestinal carcinoma, pancreatitis, cholangitis, and intestinal infarction. Colon resection and gastric resection of stomachs lacking normal acidity and motility are the elective procedures most likely to precede intraabdominal sepsis.[7-9]

Disseminated peritoneal infection depends on five factors: location and size of the primary leak; nature of the underlying injury or

FIG. 1. GasPak.

TABLE 2. GRAM-STAIN APPEARANCE OF THE COMMON ANAEROBES.[5]

Organism	Gram-negative bacilli	Gram-positive bacilli	Gram-negative cocci	Gram-positive cocci	Morphology
Actinomyces		X			Branching, filamentous
Bacteroides	X				Irregular staining, pleomorphic
Bifidobacterium		X			Bifurcated ends
Clostridium		X			Large ("box-car") or small gram-positive bacilli; spores
Eubacterium		X			Pleomorphic; no spores
Fusobacterium	X				Long, thin, often with ta-pered ends
Lactobacillus		X			Pleomorphic; long chains
Peptococcus				X	Single or clusters
Peptostreptococcus				X	Single chains
Veillonella			X		Clusters, short chains or pairs

disease; presence or absence of adhesions from previous surgery; duration of current illness; and the host's defense mechanisms.

The most frequently reported intraabdominal infection is generalized peritonitis, usually the result of penetrating or blunt abdominal trauma,[10] sometimes of organ perforation. Localized infection, or abscess, may be intraperitoneal, retroperitoneal, or visceral. Intraperitoneal abscess, usually associated with appendicitis or perforated duodenal ulcer, occurs most often in the right lower quadrant.[6] Other less frequent sites of intraabdominal abscess are the left lower quadrant and the pelvic, subphrenic, and subhepatic areas. Only rarely is it seen in the lesser sac or between the intestinal loops. Retroperitoneal abscesses, those occurring in the space between transverse fascia and peritoneum, are found about equally in the anterior and posterior spaces.[6] Posterior abscesses are usually associated with disease or trauma of the kidney, pancreas, or spine. Anterior involvement may follow surgery performed in the presence of established intraabdominal infection.

Most visceral abscesses are in the liver, although they are found infrequently in the pancreas, spleen, or kidney. Cholangitis and appendicitis account for more than 50% of liver abscesses.[10]

MICROBIOLOGY

According to the combined findings of several published studies,[6,10,11] the average number of strains of microorganisms isolated from intraabdominal infections ranges from 2.5 to 5.0, including an average of 1.4 to 2.0 aerobes and 2.4 to 3.0 anaerobes (Table 3). One or more anaerobes were isolated from 65 to 95% of patients.[6,10-12]

Commonly isolated aerobes were *Escherichia coli* and Klebsiella, Streptococcus, Proteus, and Enterobactor. Anaerobes most fre-

TABLE 3. NUMBER OF STRAINS OF MICROORGANISMS ISOLATED FROM PATIENTS WITH INTRAABDOMINAL SEPSIS IN STUDIES REPORTED FROM 1973 TO 1976.[5]

Series	No. of cases studied	Average no. of micro-organisms per infection	Average no. of aerobes per infection	Average no. of anaerobes per infection	Percent of cases with anaerobes
Altemeier et al.[6]	501	2.5	NA*	NA	65
Gorbach et al.[11]	46	5.0	2.0	3.0	87
Swenson et al.[10]	64	3.8	1.4	2.4	81
Gorbach[12]	67	4.8	1.9	2.9	94
Flora et al.[40]	73	NA	NA	NA	83

*NA = Not available.

quently seen were *Bacteroides fragilis*, the most common, Pepto-streptococcus, and Clostridium. Bacteroides species accounted for 30 to 60% of all anaerobes isolated.[10,11,13] In less than 15% of reported cases was intraabdominal sepsis found to be purely anaerobic, in 10% purely aerobic, more than 75% had mixed infections.[11,13] According to Leigh, however, he has isolated Bacteroides organisms in pure culture from more than 50% of infections associated with gastrointestinal or genitourinary disease or surgery.[14]

No association has been found between intraabdominal site of infection and type of bacteria.[15]

Based on the conclusion of Stone et al.[16] that direct exposure of the abdominal parietes to atmospheric oxygen during surgery is a major requirement for control of anaerobic bacteria isolated in peritoneal exudate, Nichols and associates have performed periodic bacteriologic studies throughout the course of a number of operations for peritonitis. Preliminary findings suggest that although the quantities of both anaerobic and aerobic species increase and decrease during any one procedure, there is no selective suppression of anaerobic bacteria by atmospheric oxygen (Figure 2).

DIAGNOSIS

Physical examination often helps to identify the involved area within the abdomen or pelvis. Diagnosis of a localized intraabdominal infection can be difficult, however. Occasionally plain films provide useful information (Figures 3 and 4) and sonography, arteriography, or radioactive scanning are often helpful in hard-to-diagnose infections (Figures 5 and 6). Bacteroides infection is strongly suggested by the finding of pleomorphic gram-negative bacilli and tentatively confirmed by failure of the organisms to grow aerobically within 48 hours.

PREVENTION

The intraabdominal sepsis associated with elective gastrointestinal surgery is preventable given good surgical techniques that minimize the spill of endogenous bacteria and the perioperative administration of appropriate wide-spectrum antibiotics. Antibiotics known to be effective against the anticipated endogenous microflora should be started preoperatively to assure adequate serum

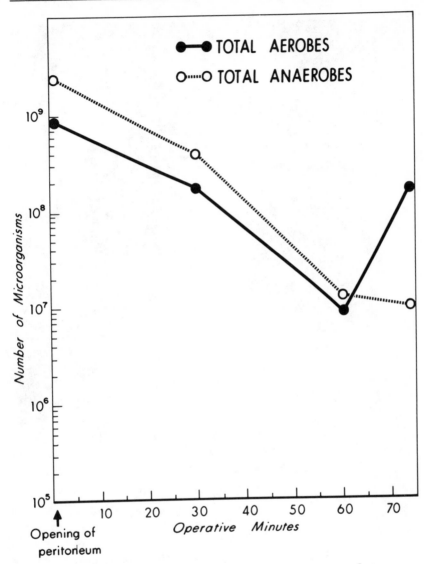

FIG. 2. Effect of atmospheric oxygen during surgery.[5]

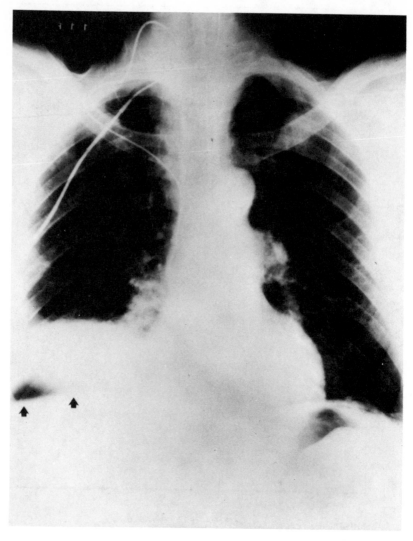

FIG. 3. Plain film provides useful information. [5]

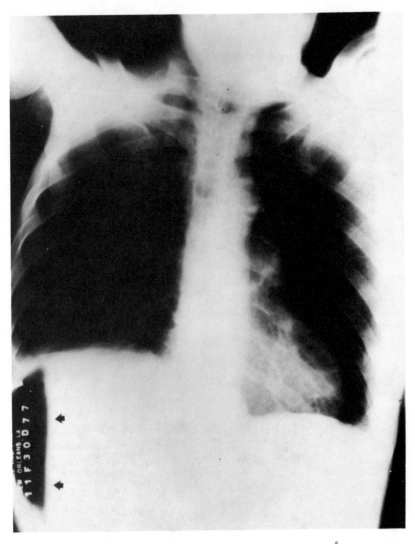

FIG. 4. Plain film provides useful information.[5]

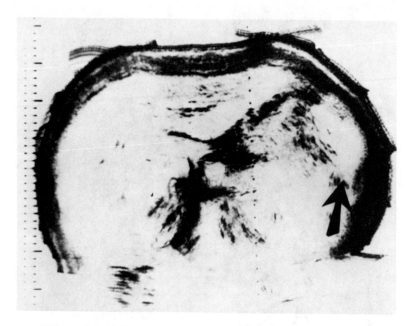

FIG. 5. Special films are helpful in hard-to-diagnose infections.[5]

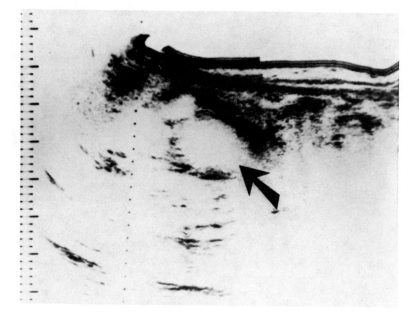

FIG. 6. Special films are helpful in hard-to-diagnose infections.[5]

levels during surgery and continued for 24 to 72 hours postoperatively.[17,18] The importance of the correct antibiotics was demonstrated in a study of prophylaxis in elective colon resection reported by Condon and his colleagues in 1979.[19] Parenteral cephalothin and oral neomycin-erythromycin base, both of which had been widely used for preoperative preparation for this procedure, were compared in a double-blind, prospective, randomized trial. Of patients given parenteral cephalothin, 39% developed postoperative sepsis, while only 6% of those treated with the oral agents had such infections. These results are not surprising, however, considering the failure of cephalothin to control *B. fragilis*, the colon's predominant anaerobe.

TREATMENT

Surgical drainage, dependent if possible, after repair or exteriorization of the involved viscera, is the primary therapy for intraabdominal sepsis. In addition, appropriate antibiotics should be administered parenterally before, during, and after drainage to prevent or reduce further local invasion and secondary septicimia with possible metastasis of the abscess.[19]

The antibiotics of choice for intraabdominal sepsis of colonic origin remain a subject for debate and of a number of clinical and experimental studies.

THE STUDIES

In most studies of antibiotics in penetrating abdominal trauma, the agents involved covered both aerobic coliforms and the anaerobic *B. fragilis* (Table 4).[16,20-22] The trial by Stone and his associates[16] of parenteral cephalothin compared with parenteral clindamycin was a major exception. Similar high infection rates in both treatment groups were probably due to the failure of both agents to control the entire spectrum of colonic flora: cephalothin has no effect on colonic anaerobes: clindamycin has no effect on the aerobes.

Most reports recommend an aminoglycoside for the aerobic gram-negative bacilli and clindamycin, chloramphenicol or metronidazole for the anaerobes, including *B. fragilis,* which is unaffected by the more common penicillins, cephalosporins, and aminoglycosides.[23]

The findings of many uncontrolled studies suggest that parenteral clindamycin is effective against severe anaerobic infec-

TABLE 4. CHOICES OF ANTIBIOTICS IN INTRAABDOMINAL SEPSIS CAUSED BY PENETRATING ABDOMINAL TRAUMA.

Authors	Recommended agents
Fullen, Hunt, and Altemeier[20]	Penicillin-tetracycline
	Penicillin-chloramphenicol
Thadepalli et al.[22]	Clindamycin-kanamycin
Stone et al.[16]	Cephalothin
O'Donnell et al.[21]	Carbenicillin

tions.[24-26] In these studies, patients have generally failed to respond to other antibiotics, such as penicillins, cephalosporins, and aminoglycosides. Surgical drainage has also been seen to fail to cure some patients, especially those with *B. fragilis* infections, who clearly need appropriate antibiotics in addition to adequate surgical intervention. Nobles,[19] Chow and Guze,[27] and Bartlett et al.[28] have all published findings confirming the importance of effective antimicrobial therapy in Bacteroides infections.

A 1979 report by Tally and associates[30] described successful treatment of polymicrobial aerobic and anaerobic intraabdominal infection with a second-generation cephalosporin, cefoxitin. This agent is the only one of the second generation cephalosporins to show such wide-spectrum activity.[29,30] The third generation cephalosporins, moxalactam, cefotaxime or cefoperazone may prove useful for mixed intraabdominal infections.

EXPERIMENTAL STUDIES

Clinical studies of therapeutic agents and approaches are seldom satisfactory, however. A number of variables simply cannot be controlled, including primary disease state, duration of illness, differences in microflora causing the sepsis and in host defenses, and use of concomitant local or parenteral antimicrobial agents. Moreover, such studies are seldom double-blind, prospective, and randomized. Thus, a number of well-controlled studies have been done to assess the effects of various antimicrobials in experimentally induced intraabdominal sepsis in rats.

In a study by Weinstein and colleagues, peritonitis was produced by inserting a capsule containing barium and rat colon contents into the animals' peritoneal cavities.[31] The untreated controls developed a two-stage disease: 37% died early of septicemia and peritonitis; all survivors, who were killed on day nine, had abdominal abscess. The group treated with antiaerobic gentamicin had a markedly reduced mortality of 4%, but 98% of survivors developed abscesses. With clindamycin therapy alone, mortality rose to 35%, but only 5% of survivors had intraabdominal abscess nine days later. Finally, combination therapy reduced early mortality to 7% and abscess to 6%, suggesting that coliform bacteria were responsible for early deaths and anaerobes for the late complications.[32]

Another study by Onderdonk and colleagues[33] implicated *E. coli* in the acute mortality and suggested that the later abscess may be the result of a synergistic relationship between anaerobic and facultative bacteria. When only *B. fragilis* was used as the inoculum, neither acute mortality nor late abscess occurred. Louis and associates[34] produced a reduction in acute mortality similar to that obtained with gentamicin when they used four cephalosporin antibiotics in the same experimental model. They also found a reduction in abscess formation with clindamycin, low-dose cefoxitin, or high-dose cephalothin.

Some of these same investigators later found that *B. fragilis fragilis*, the subspecies of *B. fragilis* most frequently isolated from clinical infections, has a polysaccharide capsule covering its outer membrane. Interestingly, this form is found in relatively low numbers in human stool compared to the other subspecies. When Onderdonk et al.[35] repeated their earlier experiment using a pure inoculum of the encapsulated *B. fragilis fragilis*, they consistently produced intraabdominal abscess. This finding suggests an association between the organism's capsule and its virulence.

Nichols and associates[36,37] then developed a second model, more closely related to human disease, using capsules containing high, moderate, and low amount of human fecal material. In untreated animals, the incidence of mortality due to peritonitis increased with increasing doses. The experiment was repeated with various commonly used antibiotics given two hours after placement of the human-stool capsules and continued for nine days. High serum levels were attained in one hour and were virtually zero six hours after intramuscular injection. Survivors were sacrificed on the tenth day.

In the high inoculum group, animals treated with either clindamycin or tobramycin alone had high early mortality. Those treated with clindamycin-tobramycin, cephalothin-tobramycin,

TABLE 5. ANTIBIOTIC AGENTS EFFECTIVE AGAINST THE AEROBIC AND ANAEROBIC COMPONENTS OF HUMAN COLONIC MICROFLORA.

Aerobic	Anaerobic
Amikacin	Clindamycin
Cefamandole	Carbenicillin, ticarcillin, pipericellin
Cefoxitin	Cefoxitin
Gentamicin	Choramphenicol
Tobramycin	Metronidazole*

Third generation cephalosporins.

cefamandole-tobramycin, or cefamandole alone showed significantly reduced early mortality. Only clindamycin-tobramycin achieved a significantly increased cure rate, however, defined as survival with no abscess at ten days. In low-inoculum groups, several antibiotics, alone or in combination, decreased mortality and increased cure rate.

Thus, it seems clear that both aerobic and anaerobic bacteria are involved in both phases of intraabdominal sepsis, a conclusion confirmed by a recent Veterans Administration study of preoperative intestinal antisepsis in patients undergoing elective colon resection.

The agents currently recommended for selective antimicrobial therapy against both aerobic coliform and anaerobic organisms in the presence of severe fecal peritonitis are listed in Table 5. Recent studies[38] have confirmed the marked effectiveness of metronidazole in treating the anaerobic component of intraabdominal infections.

SUMMARY

Intraabdominal sepsis is a frequent complication of trauma, resection, or intrinsic disease that results in intraperitoneal spillage of colon contents. Prompt, thorough surgical drainage and appropriate parenteral antibiotics aimed at both aerobic and anaerobic organisms remain the major weapons against local or diffuse sepsis and secondary septicemia.

REFERENCES

1. Altemeier WA: Bacterial flora of acute perforated appendicitis with peritonitis: Bacteriologic study based on 100 cases. Ann Surg 107:17, 1938.
2. Altemeier WA: The pathogenicity of the bacteria of appendicitis peritonitis—an experimental study. Surgery 11:374, 1942.
3. Nichols RL, Smith JW: Modern approach to the diagnosis of anaerobic surgical sepsis. Surg Clin North Am 55:21, 1975.
4. Nichols RL, Movitovhas NM, Smith JW, Balthazar E: Intraabdominal sepsis. Am Fam Phys 21:4, April 1980.
5. Nichols RL, Miller B, Smith JW: Septic complications following gastric surgery: Relationship to the endogenous gastric microflora. Surg Clin North Am 55:1367, 1975.
6. Altemeier WA, Culbertson WR, Fullen WD, et al.: Intraabdominal abscesses. Am J Surg 125:70, 1973.
7. Nichols RL, Broido P, Condon RE, et al.: Effect of preoperative neomycin-erythromycin intestinal preparation on the incidence of infectious complications following colon surgery. Ann Surg 178:453, 1973.
8. Nichols RL, Condon RE, Gorbach SL, et al.: Efficacy of preoperative antimicrobial preparation of the bowel. Ann Surg 176:227, 1972.
9. Nichols RL, Smith JW: Intragastric microbial colonization in common disease states of the stomach and duodenum. Ann Surg 182:557, 1975.
10. Swenson RM, Lorber B, Michaelson TC, et al.: The bacteriology of intraabdominal infections. Arch Surg 109:398, 1974.
11. Gorbach SL, Thadepalli H, Norsen J: Anaerobic microorganisms in intraabdominal infections. In Balows A, Dehaan RM, Dowell VR Jr, et al. (eds.): Anaerobic bacteria: Role in disease. Springfield, Charles C. Thomas, 1974.
12. Gorbach SL: Anaerobic infections: Treatment of intraabdominal sepsis. Ann Intern Med 83:377, 1975.
13. Finegold SM: Anaerobic infections of the abdomen and pelvis. Cleve Clin Q 42–113, 1975.
14. Leigh DA: Clinical importance of infections due to *Bacteroides fragilis* and role of antibiotic therapy. Br Med J 3:225, 1974.
15. Gorbach SL, Bartlett JG: Anaerobic infections (first of three parts). N Engl J Med 290:1177, 1974.
16. Stone HH, Kolb LD, Geheber CE: Incidence and significance of intraperitoneal anaerobic bacteria. Ann Surg 181:705, 1975.
17. Burke JF: The effective period of preventive antibiotic action in experimental incision and dermal lesions. Surgery 50:161, 1961.
18. Polk HC Jr, Lopez-Mayor JF: Postoperative wound infection: A prospective study of determinant factors and prevention. Surgery 66:97, 1969.
19. Nobles ER Jr: Bacteroides infections. Ann Surg 177:601, 1973.
20. Fullen WB, Hunt J, Altemeier WA: Prophylactic antibiotics in penetrating wounds of the abdomen. J Trauma 12:282, 1972.

21. O'Donnell V, Mandal AK, Lou Sister MA, et al.: Evaluation of carbenicillin and a comparison of clindamycin and gentamicin combined therapy in penetrating abdominal trauma. Surg Gynecol Obstet 147:525, 1978.
22. Thadepalli H, Gorbach SL, Broido, PW, et al.: Abdominal trauma, anaerobes, and antibiotics. Surg Gynecol Obstet 137:270, 1973.
23. Levision ME, Bran JS, Ries K: Treatment of anaerobic bacterial infections with clindamycin-2-phosphate. Antimicrob Agents Chemother 5:276, 1974.
24. Dickinson PCT, Saphyakhajon P: Treatment of Bacteroides infection with clindamycin-2-phosphate. Can Med Assoc J 111:945, 1974.
25. Fass RJ, Scholand JF, Hodges GR, et al.: Clindamycin in the treatment of serious anaerobic infections. Ann Intern Med 78:853, 1973.
26. Haldane EV, Van Rooyen CE: Treatment of severe Bacteroides infections with parenteral clindamycin. Can Med Assoc J 107:1177, 1972.
27. Chow AW, Guze LB: Bacteroidacea bacteremia: Clinical experience with 112 patients. Medicine 53:93, 1974.
28. Bartlett JG, Miao PVW: Empiric treatment with clindamycin and gentamicin of suspected sepsis due to anaerobic and aerobic bacteria. J Infect Dis 135:580, 1977.
29. Tally FP, Jacobus NV, Bartlett JG, et al.: Susceptibility of anaerobes to cefoxitin and other cephalosporins. Antimicrob Agents Chemother 7:128, 1975.
30. Tally FP, Miao OVW, O'Keefe JP, et al.: Cefoxitin therapy of anaerobic and aerobic infections. J Antimicrob Chemo 5:101, 1979.
31. Weinstein WM, Onderdonk AB, Bartlett JG, et al.: Experimental intraabdominal abscesses in rats. Development of an experimental model. Infect Immun 10:1250, 1974.
32. Weinstein WM, Onderdonk AB, Bartlett JG, et al.: Antimicrobial therapy of experimental intraabdominal sepsis. J Infect Dis 132:282, 1975.
33. Onderdonk AB, Bartlett JG, Louis T, et al.: Microbial synergy in experimental intraabdominal abscess. Infect Immun 13:22, 1976.
34. Louis TJ, Onderdonk AB, Gorbach SL, et al.: Therapy for experimental intraabdominal sepsis. Comparisons of four cephalosporins with clindamycin plus gentamicin. J Infect Dis 135(Suppl):S18, 1977.
35. Onderdonk AB, Kasper DL, Cisneros RL, et al.: The capsular polysaccharide of *Bacteroides fragilis* as a virulence factor: Comparison of the pathogenic potential of encapsulated and unencapsulated strains. J Infect Dis 136:82, 1977.
36. Nichols RL, Smith JW, Balthazar ER: Peritonitis and intraabdominal abscess: An experimental model for the evaluation of human disease. J Surg Res 25:129, 1978.
37. Nichols RL, Smith JW, Fossedal EN, et al.: Efficacy of parenteral antibiotics in the treatment of experimental induced intraabdominal sepsis. Rev Infect Dis 1:302, 1979.

38. Stone HH, Fabian TC: Clinical comparison of antibiotic combinations in the treatment of peritonitis and related mixed aerobic-anaerobic surgical sepsis. World J Surg 4:415, 1980.
39. Bartlett J: Metronidazole. Johns Hopkins Med J 149:89–92, August, 1981.
40. Flora D, Finegold SM: Personal communication.

CHAPTER THREE

Intraabdominal Abscess: Pathogenesis and Antibiotic Selection

John G. Bartlett, M.D.

Three aspects of intraabdominal abscesses will be discussed: The role of various bacteria at the infected site, the choice of antibiotics and the important principal of early institution of appropriate agents. Most of the information provided is based on animal studies, but we believe the questions posed and the results obtained provide guidelines for the management of patients.

First I would like to review a case in order to provide a reference source for some of the points of emphasis. The patient was admitted with a left subphrenic abscess which was surgically drained. Purulent material obtained at the operation was aspirated into a syringe which was delivered promptly to the microbiology laboratory where a Gram stain showed numerous morphotypes indicating a polymicrobial flora. The specimen was processed using optimal microbiological techniques and the following organisms where recovered: *E. coli*, *Klebsiella pneumoniae*, *Proteus mirabilis*, *B. fragilis*, *Clostridium perfringens*, *C. bifermentans*, *C. barati*, *C. innocuum*, *Peptostreptococcus anaerobius*, *Peptococcus prevotii*, *Eubacterium multiforme*, *E. lentum*, and *Veillonella parvula*. This patient received antibiotics selected empirically prior to the surgical drainage procedure and was well on the way to recovery when the bacteriology report showing these results was received. The following points in this case deserve emphasis:

1. The number and types of bacteria recovered in intraabdominal sepsis is largely dependent on the quality of the microbiology performed. This specimen was processed in a research laboratory, but most clinical laboratories do not have the time or resources for an analysis which detected 13 different species. Given the same specimen, many laboratories would recover only certain aerobes, a more industrious effort might uncover some anaerobes, and skilled technicians with unlimited resources would probably detect even more organisms.
2. Antibiotic decisions in cases of intraabdominal sepsis usually require decisions based on anticipated pathogens rather than the culture report. The problem is that specimens from the infected site are often not available; even when they are obtained, there are often extensive time delays before results are available and limited resources commonly result in incomplete studies.
3. The types of organisms recovered in this case were largely predictable on the basis of multiple studies of intraabdominal sepsis which provide the guidelines for the empiric decisions which are necessary.

BACTERIOLOGY

Most cases of intraabdominal sepsis involve the colonic microflora. The colon harbors bacteria in concentrations approaching 10^{12}/g which approximates the geometric limits with which these organisms can occupy space. In other words, the dry weight of stool is almost entirely bacteria. It is a very complex flora with estimates of up to 400 or 500 species of bacteria. The dominate forms are anaerobes which account for over 99% of the cultivable flora. The flora of the stomach and the small bowel of healthy individuals harbor substantially lower numbers of bacteria and the flora is considerably less complex. The prevalence of colonic bacteria in intraabdominal sepsis is presumably related to the inoculum size, and the associated conditions which cause a breach in mucosal integrity, such as appendicitis, diverticulitis, carcinoma of the colon, inflammatory bowel disease, and prior surgery on the colon.

Several years ago, we reviewed the bacteriology of 72 patients[1] who had intraabdominal sepsis including either generalized peritonitis or intraabdominal abscesses (Table 1). As expected,

TABLE 1. BACTERIOLOGY IN 72 CASES OF INTRAABDOMINAL SEPSIS (MAJOR ISOLATES).

Aerobic bacteria		Anerobic bacteria	
E. coli	40	*B. fragilis* group	62
Proteus sp	18	Clostridia sp	45
Klebsiella sp	16	Eubacteria	23
Pseudomonas sp	11	Peptostreptococci	19
Enterobacter sp	9	Fusobacteria	17
Enterococcus	10	*B. melaninogenicus*	13
		Peptococci	8

nearly all of these infections involved a polymicrobial flora, there being an average of 5 microbial species per specimen, including three anaerobic species and two aerobic species. These results are not surprising in view of the complexity of the inoculum. These results are also not unique since similar findings were reported in the very first reort of the bacteriology of intraabdominal sepsis in which anaerobic cultures were performed in 1897.[2] Our study, like similar studies utilizing optimal bacteriological techniques, showed that the most common aerobic bacteria recovered was *E. coli* and the most frequent anaerobe recovered was *Bacteroides fragilis*.

The complexity of the flora at the infected site makes it difficult to determine which of these organisms are true pathogens and which are symbionts or commensals.[3] This issue poses very important and practical questions since it determines, to a large extent, the principles for antibiotic selection. One view is that anaerobic bacteria are the dominant forms, are the major pathogens and should be the exclusive target of therapy.[4,5] Another view is that anaerobes survive at the infected site only because aerobic bacteria produce the appropriate environmental milleux to permit their survival; thus, elimination of the aerobes should be the major goal.[6,7] Unfortunately, clinical studies have provided only partial and unconvincing data to support or refute these diametrically opposed positions.

ANIMAL MODEL OF INTRAABDOMINAL SEPSIS

An animal model was established in order to examine the role of various bacteria in these types of infections.[8-12] Wistar rats were challenged with an inoculum composed of pooled stool which was placed in gelatin capsules for insertion into the abdominal cavity in an attempt to simulate the septic complications which follow colonic perforation. The initial work was designed to describe the pathologic changes and bacteriology at the infected site in animals which were sequentially killed (Table 2). These studies showed a two-stage infection, now referred to as the biphasic disease process.[8,9] During the first phase, there was a free flowing exudate representing generalized peritonitis. The second phase was characterized by intraabdominal abscesses which were detected in all animals killed after seven days. There was a 43% natural mortality and all deaths occurred during the first five days following challenge, e.g., during the generalized peritonitis stage. These observations have been consistent in studies of the model in over a thousand animals during a five-year study period. This may reflect the use of a uniform inoculum, similar animals and standardized methods of evaluation. However, the clinical counterparts to this biphasic disease in patients may show considerable variations depending on the host, the inoculum size, and defense mechanisms. In many instances, the inoculum is restricted to the site of entry resulting in a "phlegmon" or localized peritonitis. At the other end of the spectrum is acute generalized peritonitis with a fulminant course, large fluid collections in the abdomen, and shock. With either localized or generalized peritonitis, the long-term sequelae is abdominal abscess formation. These abscesses may be localized to the area of a

TABLE 2. RAT MODEL OF INTRAABDOMINAL SEPSIS.

	No. rats	Peritonitis stage	Abscess stage
Time after challenge		1–5 days	7–14 days
Pathologic findings	283	Free flowing exudate	Loculated abscesses
Mortality rate	283	39%	0
Bacteriology			
Blood cultures	30	E. coli (93%)	Negative
Exudate*	20	E. coli (6.2)	B. fragilis (8.8)
		B. fragilis (6.0)	F. varium (8.6)
		Enterococcus	E. coli (7.7)
		(5.0)	Enterococcus (5.7)

*Organisms noted were present in all specimens and are listed in rank order with median concentrations in parenthesis expressed as $\log_{10}$/ml.

preceding phlegmon (e.g., periappendiceal abscess of diverticular abscess) or the abscesses may be remote from the portal of entry. In the latter instance, the favored locations are subphrenic or subhepatic as a result of caudad flow due to negative intrathoracic pressure or localization in the pelvis or paracolic gutter reflecting gravitational flow.[13]

Bacteriological studies of exudate from the infected site showed similar qualitative results during both the generalized peritonitis and abscess stages of this infection. As with patients, there was a polymicrobial flora. *E. coli, enterococci,* and *B. fragilis* were universally present, but there were differences between these bacteria according to quantitative analysis. The numerically dominant organism in peritonitis exudate during the early phase of the infection was *E. coli.* More importantly, blood cultures obtained during this early phase of the infection yielded *E. coli* in 93% of the animals. By contrast, the numerically dominant organism in abscesses was *B. fragilis* with mean counts of 10^9/ml of exudate. These results suggested that coliform bacteremia was responsible for the early mortality associated with acute peritonitis whereas *Bacteroides fragilis* appeared to be particularly important during the abscess stage.

Impressions regarding the relative roles of coliforms in anaerobic bacteria were subsequently supported in another study using selective antibiotic therapy.[10] In this experiment, clindamycin or gentamicin were administered beginning four hours after challenge. The selection of these drugs was based on their restricted spectrum of activity, gentamicin being active against coliforms but inactive against anaerobic bacteria while clindamycin has the opposite spectrum. The results of this experiment showed that gentamicin reduced the natural mortality rate from 43% to 4%, although 54 of 55 (98%) surviving animals had typical intraabdominal abscesses. Clindamycin had no important effect on reducing mortality rates, but did reduce the incidence of abscesses to only 5%.

An additional experiment was done to further identify the role of various bacteria in this infection by challenging the animals with the organisms which were recovered from infected sites in pure culture rather than using the inoculum of stool (Table 3). This experiment showed that *E. coli* (and presumably other coliforms as well) were the only organisms which caused acute death and the mortality rate was directly correlated with the inoculum size.[11] *B. fragilis* was the only organism examined which caused abscess formation. Thus, three experimental procedures were used to define the role of various bacteria in this two-stage infection: sequential

TABLE 3. MONOMICROBIAL CHALLENGE IN INTRAABDOMINAL SEPSIS MODEL.

Organism	Inoculum size (log_{10})	Mortality rate	Incidence of abscesses
E. coli	7.8	20/20 (100%)	—
	7.4	13/20 (65%)	0/7
	7.1	6/20 (30%)	0/14
	6.8	0/20	0/20
Enterococcus	7.8	0/20	0/20
F. varium	7.8	0/20	0/20
B. fragilis			
Unencapsulated	7.8	0/20	0/20
Encapsulated	7.8	0/20	19/20 (95%)
Capsular polysaccharide	100 mcg	0/10	5/10 (50%)
	200 mcg	0/8	8/8 (100%)

studies of bacteriology, results of antimicrobial probes, and monomicrobial challenge. All of these experiments supported the conclusion that coliforms were primarily responsible for the acute lethality which occurred in the early stages of generalized peritonitis while anaerobic bacteria, especially B. fragilis, appeared to play a decisive role in abscess formation. It might be important to mention that enterococci, a rather controversial organism in intraabdominal sepsis, did not appear to play any well defined role in this infection according to the studies with antibiotics or with challenge using this organism in pure culture.

BACTEROIDES FRAGILIS

Bacteroides fragilis is an organism of particular interest in intraabdominal sepsis due to a long standing controversy regarding pathogenic potential. This organism is frequently recovered from blood cultures in patients with intraabdominal sepsis and it is the most frequent isolate from exudate in these cases.[1,14] Nevertheless, some authorities doubt any pathogenic role based largely on experiments of acute mortality in experimental animals. Our studies and those of other workers indicate that B. fragilis does not cause acute lethality when injected intraperitoneally or intraveneously in several different animal species.[11,15] A likely explanation for the difference with this organism compared to *E. coli* concerns the biological activity and chemical composition of endotoxin. The endotoxin of *B. fragilis* differs from that of coliforms in that it lacks heptose, KDO, and beta-hydroxy miristic acid.[16] More importantly, although positive in the limulus lysate test, the endotoxin of *B. fragilis* is negative in the chick embryo death test using a concentration of 100 times that necessary to elicit a positive response by *S. typhi* and it gives a negative Shwartzman reaction with concentrations of up to one milligram. This provides a presumptive explanation for the lack of hypotension, lethality, and other acute events which are characteristically seen with coliform bacteremia. The results cited here appeared to show a well defined role for *B. fragilis* in the later stage of the biphasic disease in which there was abscess formation.

At the time this work was done, Kasper at the Channing Laboratory in Boston was performing studies to characterize the cell wall constituents of *B. fragilis* which resulted in the observation noted in the preceding paragraph regarding the endotoxin.[16] Kasper also noted that some strains of *B. fragilis* contained a polysaccharide capsule which is external to the outer membrane. At the time of this work, studies in other laboratories using DNA homology showed that the organisms previously classified as subspecies of *B. fragilis* were actually distinct species.[17] The encapsulated forms were *B. fragilis* ss *fragilis* which has now been reclassified as *B. fragilis;* the other subspecies were given species rank and all are included in the umbrella appellation *"B. fragilis* group." The potential clinical relevance of this observation concerns the fact that analysis of stool, which serves as the presumed portal of entry for most cases of intraabdominal sepsis, showed that the encapsulated strains of *Bacteroides fragilis* comprise a relatively small portion of the fecal flora,[18] although this organism represents the most frequent isolate at infected sites.[19] The disproportionate ratio between concentrations in the colon and frequency of recovery at infected sites supported the notion that the capsule represents a virulence factor. This possibility was examined in the animal model by comparing inocula composed of encapsulated and unencapsulated strains of *B. fragilis.*[13] It was noted that abscesses were produced only with the encapsulated strains. Of particular interest was the observation that abscesses were produced using a challenge of *B. fragilis-*capsular polysaccharide alone. The abscesses in these animals appeared similar to those noted using an inoculum of stool except that exudate showed no bacteria on Gram stain and cultures were sterile. This work indicates a rather unique property for *B. fragilis* for promoting abscess formation.

ANTIBIOTIC SELECTION

The conclusion from the series of experiments described in previous section is that both coliforms and anaerobes, especially *B. fragilis,* appear to represent pathogens in the septic events which commonly follow colonic perforation. However, they appear to play somewhat different roles as the infection evolves through the two stages of acute peritonitis with early lethality followed by the second stage characterized by abscess formation. If these conclusions are correct, optimal antibiotic therapy should be directed at both coliforms and anaerobes. In many instances, this results in a two-drug combination including an aminoglycoside and a second drug with activity against *B. fragilis.*

There are six antimicrobial agents which are advocated for *B. fragilis:* clindamycin, cefoxitin, chloramphenicol, carbenicillin, moxalactam, and metronidazole. Clinical trials comparing these drugs have shown no important difference in relative efficacy.[20-23] It is our impression that these studies suffer from several disadvantages, the most important being the fact that surgery often represents the most important therapeutic modality and because the end points used to judge outcome are relatively crude. Thus, animal models become an attractive method to comparative efficacy. The intraabdominal sepsis model was utilized to examine 29 different antimicrobial regimens using two parameters to judge in vivo activity: prevention of early lethality and the incidence of abscesses in surviving animals. This work supported the previous conclusions that regimens which included an agent active against coliforms reduced mortality rates, agents active against *B. fragilis* prevented abscesses, and regimens with activity against both components produced the highest cure rates.[24] However, no important difference was noted in the incidence of abscesses for five of the six agents active against *B. fragilis* in vitro. Problems with this model for examining antibiotic in vivo activity against this organism are that the infection involves multiple microbes so that attention could not be focused entirely on *B. fragilis,* all animals received a standardized challenge so that only one strain of *B. fragilis* was examined, and there was no way to quantitate results so that multiple therapeutic regimens appeared to be equally meritorious. For these reasons, another more refined model was established with mice challenged subcutaneously with an inoculum composed of multiple strains of *B. fragilis* in pure culture combined with autoclaved cecal contents. Studies of untreated animals showed all developed loculated subcutaneous abscesses within five days.[25] To test antimicrobials, therapy was initiated one hour after challenge, and the drugs were given at eight-hour intervals for a period of five days. The results were evaluated by a quantitative culture of extirpated abscesses to determine the number of viable organisms which remained at the infected site at the completion of treatment. Fifteen clinical isolates of B. fragilis were tested utilizing the six drugs noted earlier as well as cephalothin in order to have a commonly used antibiotic which is relatively inactive in vitro against these organisms.[26] A desirable feature of this model is that the results could be quantitated to provide a sensitive measure of relative in vivo activity.

The mean number of bacteria per abscess in untreated animals was $10^{9.9}$. The best activity of the antibiotics tested was achieved with metronidazole which reduced the mean count for the 15 strains by over $10^{6.7}$ (Table 4). (The "greater than" designation is necessary because many of these animals had no bacteria recovered and were arbitrarily assigned a concentration of $10^{1.7}$ since this is the smallest number bacteria which can be detected with our techniques.) Clindamycin produced a five log decrease compared to untreated controls, while cefoxitin and moxalactam reduced counts by $10^{3.8}$ and $10^{3.5}$, respectively. Chloramphenicol was significantly less effective in this model as it was in our previous studies utilizing this drug in the intraabdominal abscess model.[24] Chloramphenicol is almost uniformly active against B. fragilis in vitro, although the poor results noted here for in vivo activity have also been noted by others utilizing alternative animal models.[27,28] One possible explanation for

TABLE 4. COMPARATIVE EFFICACY OF ANTIMICROBIAL AGENTS VERSUS BACTEROIDES FRAGILIS IN MOUSE MODEL.

	Decrease in count*	Statistical analysis**
Metronidazole	> 6.7 ± 0.6	1
Clindamycin	5.0 ± 0.6	2
Moxalactam	3.8 ± 0.6	2, 3
Cefoxitin	3.5 ± 0.5	3
Chloramphenicol	1.6 ± 0.5	4
Carbenicillin	1.0 ± 0.3	4, 5
Cephalothin	0.4 ± 0.2	5

*Mean decrease (± SEM) for 15 strains expressed as $\log_{10}$.
**Results for agents with same numerical designation are not significantly different (t-test independent means, $p > 0.05$).

the discrepancy between in vivo activity in animals and the favorable in vitro activity concerns the fact that *B. fragilis* may inactivate the drug by reduction of the nitro group. This is a slow inactivation process which is optimally demonstrated using a large inoculum size.[28] It is not known if these in vitro and in vivo observations have direct clinical relevance, although we have anecdotally noted a number of clinical failures with chloramphenicol among patients with *B. fragilis* bacteremia in which this drug failed to eliminate the organism from the blood stream.[29] Carbenicillin was relatively inactive in this animal model, possibly reflecting its often marginal activity against *B. fragilis*. As expected, cephalothin showed no significant reduction in bacterial counts compared to untreated control animals.

TIMING OF ANTIBIOTICS

Its seems intuitively obvious that early institution of appropriate antibiotic therapy should provide optimal results. This was elegantly demonstrated in the work of Burke and Miles in their classical studies of staphylococcal infections in experimental animals.[30] These investigators showed that a progressive delay in the institution of antibiotics was accompanied by a substantial reduction in the impact of these agents as determined by lesion size. The interval between challenge and any demonstrable effect was defined as the "decisive interval," which for *S. aureus* in the model they tested was only three hours.

Similar studies were conducted by our group utilizing the previously described model of a soft tissue abscess involving with *B. fragilis*. Two different parameters were evaluated: the pharmacokinetic profile of drugs for relative ability to penetrate abscesses and the effect of drugs on counts of *B. fragilis* with delayed treatment. In the penetration study, antibiotics were not initiated until abscesses had formed at five days.[31] At that time, 3 doses were administered at 8-hour intervals and the animals were then sacrificed at intervals of 0, 10, 15, 30, 60, and 120 minutes to obtain levels of the antibiotic in both serum and abscess contents. This work showed that all antibiotics penetrated well into abscesses to provide peak levels which were generally 20−50% of the mean peak serum levels. Thus, all of these drugs appeared to penetrate into abscesses to provide concentrations which generally exceeded the minimum inhibitory concentration. It was also noted that no detectable levels were obtained prior to the third dose and the pharmacokinetic profile within the abscess reflected the concurrent serum profile except that the peak was somewhat delayed and the half-life was somewhat prolonged. This indicates rather free ingress and egress into the abscess despite the lack of a vascular supply and the presence of a thick collagen wall.

The second experiment in this model was to initiate therapy at various intervals following challenge in order to define the "decisive interval" as previously described for *S. aureus* by Burke and Miles. With clindamycin and cefoxitin, there was a gradual diminution in the extent to which viable counts were reduced with a progressive delay in therapy. With both of these drugs, the decrease in bacterial counts following a five-day course initiated at five days after challenge was only about one log.[26] By contrast (Figure 1), metronidazole had a sustained impact on the counts of bacteria at the infected site irrespective of the time that antibiotic treatment was initiated. Similar results have been noted by Wells and Wilkins as well.[32] Our interpretation of these results is that it reflects the somewhat unique activity of metronidazole against *B. fragilis*. Time kill curves indicate that this is the only antibiotic which is rapidly bactericidal against *B. fragilis*.[33] The biological activity of metronidazole appears to be mediated by transitory products produced ₔuring reduction of the 5-nitro group. This reduction activation

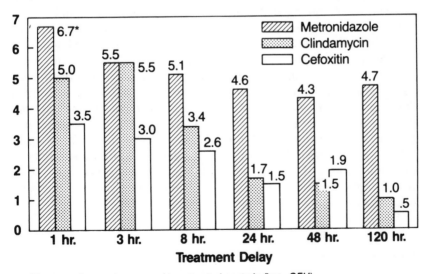

*Decrease in count compared to untreated controls (log_{10} CFU).

FIG. 1. Critical interval in treatment of experimental *Bacteroides fragilis* infection.

requires metabolic activity, but not replication. Alternative antimicrobials are active primarily against *B. fragilis* during logarhythmic growth. The difference in in vivo activity between drugs when initiated after abscesses have already formed may reflect the fact that bacteria within an abscess are in a relatively stationary growth phase.

A conclusion from these studies is that management principles vary considerably with different stages of infections. These may be divided into three phases: prevention or prophylaxis, treatment during an evolving infection ("the critical interval"), and management after an abscess has formed. For prophylaxis, drugs are given prior to an established infection, and the guidelines regarding the use of antimicrobials are quite different compared to those for the management of an established infection. Witness, for example, the utility of orally administered erythromycin and neomycin which have proven to be so successful in the prevention of postoperative infections following elective colon surgery.[34] This regimen could not be recommended for the management of intraabdominal sepsis. Similar observations apply to gynecologic surgery in which multiple penicillins, cephalosporins, and other drugs all appear to be equally effective. Once the infection has taken place, the guidelines are really quite different. For most drugs, optimal results are achieved during the early stage of the infection defined as the "critical interval." It is during this phase of the infection that the physician has the optimal opportunity to eradicate the infection with antibiotics. The point has been emphasized that empirical decisions are generally required since one does not have the luxury or levity of awaiting results from the microbiology laboratory. For intraabdominal sepsis, this can usually be done utilizing information derived from numerous studies which show stereotyped patterns of bacteria with rather predictable susceptibility profiles. Once an abscess has formed, it generally requires drainage and the role of antibiotics appears to be primarily adjunctive. The somewhat unique activity of metronidazole with abscesses involving *B. fragilis* has been illustrated in the animal model, although this observation has not been confirmed in clinical studies.

REFERENCES

1. Gorbach SL: Treatment of intraabdominal sepsis. Ann Intern Med 83:377–379, 1975.
2. Veillcn A, Zuber A: Sur quelques microbes strictment anaerobies et

leur role dans la pathologie humaine. CR Soc Biol (Paris) 49:253–255, 1897.

3. Gorbach SL, Bartlett JG: Anaerobic infections: Old myths and new realities. J Infect Dis 130:307–310, 1974.

4. Willis AT, Ferguson IR, Jones PH, et al.: Metronidazole in prevention and treatment of bacteroides infections in elective colonic surgery. Brit Med J 1:607–610, 1977.

5. Ingham HR, Selkon JB, Roxby CM: Bacteriological study of otogenic cerebral abscesses: Chemotherapeutic role of metronidazole. Brit Med J 2:991–993, 1977.

6. Stone HH, Kolb LD, Geheber CE: Incidence and significance of intraperitoneal anaerobic bacteria. Amer Surg 181:705–715, 1975.

7. Fry DE: Anaerobes and intraabdominal infections: A skeptic's viewpoint. Management of surgical infections. Kerstein MD (Editor) Futura Publ Co, Mt Kisco, NY, 1980, pp. 107–113.

8. Weinstein WM, Onderdonk AB, Bartlett JB, Gorbach SL: Experimental intraabdominal abscesses in rats: I. Development of an experimental model. Infect Immun 10:1250–1255, 1974.

9. Onderdonk AB, Weinstein WM, Sullivan NM, Bartlett JG, Gorbach SL: Experimental intraabdominal abscesses in rats: II. Quantitative bacteriology of infected animals. Infect Immun 10:1256–1259, 1974.

10. Weinstein WM, Onderdonk AB, Bartlett JG, Gorbach SL: Antimicrobial therapy of experimental intraabdominal sepsis. J Infect Dis 132:282–286, 1975.

11. Onderdonk AB, Bartlett JG, Louie TJ, Sullivan-Sigler N, Gorbach SL: Microbial synergy in experimental intraabdominal abscess. Infect Immun 13:22–26, 1976.

12. Onderdonk AB, Kasper DL, Bartlett JG: The capsular polysaccharide of B. fragilis as a virulence factor: Comparison of the pathogenic potential of encapsulated and unencapsulated strains. J Infect Dis 136:82–89, 1977.

13. Altemeier WA, Culbertson WR, Fullen WD, et al.: Intraabdominal abscesses. Amer J Surg 125:70, 1973.

14. Bartlett JG, Condon RE, Gorbach SL, Clarke JS, Nichols RL, Ochi S: Veterans Administration Cooperative Study on bowel preparation for elective colon surgery. Ann Surg 188:126–131, 1978.

15. O'Donnell TF Jr, Connolly RA, Gorbach SL, Tally FP: The circulatory effects of an acute infusion of anaerobes in a rabbit model. Surg Gynec Obstet 151:735–739, 1980.

16. Kasper DL: Chemical and biological characterization of lipopolysaccharide of Bacteroides fragilis. J Infect Dis 134:59, 1976.

17. Cato EP, Johnson JL: Reinstatement of species rank for Bacteroides fragilis, B. distasonis, B. thetaiotaomicron and B. vulgatus: Designation of neotype strains for Bacteroides fragilis (Veillon and Zuber) Castellani and Chalmers and Bacteroides thetaiotaomicron (Distaso) Castellani and Chalmers. Internat J Syst Bacteriol 26:230–237, 1976.

18. Moore WEC: Anaerobes as normal flora: Gastrointestinal tract. In

62   J.G. BARTLETT

Metronidazole, Finegold SM ed. Excerpta Medica, Princeton, NJ, 1977, pp. 222–228.
19. Polk BF, Kasper DL: *Bacteroides fragilis* subspecies in clinical isolates. Ann Intern Med 86:569–571, 1977.
20. Smith JA, Skidmore AG, Forward AD, et al.: Prospective, randomized, double-blind comparison of metronidazole and tobramycin with clindamycin and tobramycin in the treatment of intraabdominal sepsis. Ann Surg 192:213–220, 1980.
21. Klastersky J, Coppens L, Mombelli G: Anaerobic infection in cancer patients: Comparative evaluation of clindamycin and cefoxitin. Antimicrob Ag Chemother 6:366–371, 1979.
22. Harding GKM, Buckwold FJ, Ronald AR, et al.: Prospective randomized comparative study of clindamycin, chloramphenicol, and ticarcillin, each in combination with gentamicin in therapy for intraabdominal and female genital tract sepsis. J Infect Dis 142:384–393, 1980.
23. Tally FP, McGowan K, Kellum JM, Gorbach SL, O'Donnell TF: A randomized comparison of cefoxitin with or without amikacin and clindamycin plus amikacin in surgical sepsis. Ann Surg 193:318–323, 1981.
24. Bartlett JG, Louie TJ, Gorbach SL, Onderdonk AB: Therapeutic efficacy of 29 microbial regimens in experimental intraabdominal sepsis. Rev Infec Dis 3:535–542, 1981.
25. Joiner KA, Onderdonk AB, Gelfand JA, Bartlett JG, Gorbach SL: A quantitative model for subcutaneous abscess formation in mice. Brit J Exper Path 61:97–107, 1980.
26. Joiner K, Lowe B, Dzink J, Bartlett JG: Comparative efficacy of ten antimicrobial agents in experimental *Bacteroides fragilis* infections. J Infect Dis (in press).
27. Walker CB, Nitzan D, Wilkins TD: Chemotherapy of an experimental *Bacteroides fragilis* infection in mice. Antimicrob Ag Chemother 11:435–440, 1977.
28. Onderdonk AB, Kasper DL, Mansheim BJ, Louie TJ, Gorbach SL, Bartlett JG: Experimental animal models for anaerobic infections. Rev Infec Dis 1:291–301, 1979.
29. Thadepalli H, Gorbach SL, Bartlett JG: Apparent failure of chloramphenicol in anaerobic infections. Curr Therap Res 22:421–426, 1977.
30. Burke JF: The effective period of preventive antibiotic action in experimental incisions and dermal lesions. Surgery 50:161–168, 1961.
31. Joiner KA, Lowe BR, Dzink JL, Bartlett JG: Antibiotic levels in infected and sterile subcutaneous abscesses in mice. J Infect Dis 143:487–494, 1981.
32. Wells CL, Wilkins TD: Bactericidal effect of metronidazole in mixed-flora abscesses containing anaerobic and facultative bacteria. Current Chemotherapy and Infectious Disease. Amer Soc Microbiol Washington DC, 1980, pp. 892–893.
33. Ralph ED, Kirby WM: Unique bactericidal action of metronidazole

against *Bacteroides fragilis* and *Clostridium perfringens.* Antimicrob Ag Chemother 8:409–414, 1975.
34. Clarke JS, Condon RE, Bartlett JG, Gorbach SL, Nichols RL, Ochi S: Preoperative oral antibiotics reduce septic complications of colorectal operations: Results of prospective, randomized, double-blind clinical study. Ann Surg 186:251–258, 1977.

CHAPTER FOUR

Bacterial Synergy, Virulence Factors, and Host Defense Mechanisms in the Pathogenesis of Intraabdominal Infections

H. Stephen Bjornson, M.D., Ph.D.

INTRODUCTION

With improvements in anaerobic culture technology during the last decade, there has been renewed awareness of the importance of anaerobic bacteria in surgical infections. Anaerobic bacteria constitute the predominant part of the normal indigenous microflora. Anaerobes outnumber facultative and aerobic bacteria by a factor of 1000 to 1 in the colon; in the mouth, skin, upper respiratory, and female genitourinary tracts, this ratio ranges from 10–100 to 1.[1-3] Infections encountered by the surgeon usually result from perturbation of mucous membranes at the site of surgery, trauma, or disease. In most cases, bacteriological studies have documented the involvement of multiple facultative and anaerobic bacterial species of the indigenous microflora in the proximate area.[4,5] The purpose of this paper is to review current knowledge of synergistic interactions between facultative and anaerobic bacteria in polymicrobic infections, virulence factors of gram-negative anaerobic bacilli, and mechanisms of host resistance against these bacteria.

SYNERGY

Synergistic interactions among bacteria in mixed infections appear to play an important role in the disease process. Synergy may be defined as the cooperative interaction of two or more bacterial species that produces a result not achieved by the individual bacteria acting alone. One of the earliest descriptions of bacterial synergy was reported by Brewer and Melony in 1926.[6] These investigators described a spreading gangrene of the abdominal wall complicating drainage of appendiceal abscesses in two patients. *Staphylococcus aureus* and a nonhemolytic microaerophilic streptococcus were isolated from the wound of one of the patients. When either isolate was injected subcutaneously into rabbits, guinea pigs, or dogs, no lesion resulted. Inoculation of a mixture of the bacteria produced a spreading gangrenous infection involving the skin and subcutaneous tissues which simulated the infection observed in man.

Synergy between facultative and anaerobic bacteria in experimental infection has been demonstrated using various animal models (Table 1). Pure cultures of facultative and anaerobic bacteria isolated from human and animal sources generally failed to produce infection. However, mixtures of the bacteria elicited necrotizing infections which were characterized by a mixed bacterial flora in which anaerobes were numerically dominant. The demonstration of bacterial synergy is in sharp contrast to the "one microorganism—one disease" concept that characterizes most infectious processes.

Minimal information is available regarding the mechanisms responsible for the observed synergistic interactions in mixed bacterial infections. Several investigators have suggested that facultative bacteria lower the oxidation-reduction potential of tissues and thereby facilitate the growth of anaerobes. Roberts studied synergistic interactions of *Fusobacterium necrophorus* and *Corynebacterium pyogenes*; together these microorganisms cause ovine footabscess.[16,17] *F. necrophorus* was shown to produce a leukocidal exotoxin which protected both *C. pyogenes* and itself from

**TABLE 1. ANIMAL MODELS OF
SYNERGISTIC INFECTIONS INVOLVING
ANAEROBES.**

Reference	Source of bacterial isolates	Animal
Altemeier[7]	Peritonitis secondary to perforated appendicitis*	Guinea pig
Hite et al.[8]	Female genital tract*	White mice
Rosebury et al.[9,10]	Gingival crevice*	Guinea pig
MacDonald et al.[11-13]	Gingival crevice*	Guinea pig
Socransky and Gibbons[14]	Gingival crevice, human feces*	Guinea pig
Hampp and Mergenhagen[15]	Oral cavity*	Rabbit
Roberts[16,17]	infective bulbar necrosis of sheep	Guinea pig, rabbit
Egerton et al.[18,19]	Ovine foot-rot	Sheep
Weinstein et al.[20]	Rat cecal contents	Rat
Onderdonk et al.[21]	Rat cecal contents	Rat
Lykkegaard Nielsen et al.[22]	Intraabdominal abscess*	Rabbit
Kelly[23]	N.C.T.C.†	Guinea pig

*Human isolates.
†Isolates obtained from the National Collection of Type Cultures.

phagocytosis. *C. pyogenes* was shown to produce a factor which stimulated the growth of *F. necrophorus*. MacDonald et al. investigated the interactions among *Bacteroides melaninogenicus* and three other bacteria isolated from gingival crevice scrapings in an experimental mixed infection in guinea pigs.[13] These investigators demonstrated that one of the bacteria in the mixed infection, a facultative diphtheroid, produced naphthoquinone, a required growth factor for *B. melaninogenicus*.

Another form of interaction between bacteria that can be detrimental to the host is the protection of one species by another from the action of antibiotics. Several investigators have demonstrated the production of β-lactamase by strains of *B. fragilis* in vitro and in vivo.[24-26] The presence of *B. fragilis* in a mixed infection may reduce

68 H.S. BJORNSON

the effectiveness of β-lactam antibiotics and thus protect other bacterial species from the antibiotic.

VIRULENCE FACTORS

Gram-negative anaerobic bacilli have been shown to produce a variety of enzymes that have the potential to damage host tissue. Table 2 summarizes the enzymes which have been demonstrated in cultures of Bacteroides. It has been suggested that heparinase produced by several strains of the B. fragilis group may play a role in the pathogenesis of deep vein thrombosis, a complication which has been associated with Bacteroides bacteremia.[28,33,34] Collagenase produced by B. melaninogenicus may be important as a cause of bone resorption in periodontal disease.[13,31,35] Superoxide dismutase may permit pathogenic anaerobes to survive in oxygenated tissues until the proper reduced conditions for their growth are established.[32] The precise role of these and other enzymes in the pathogenesis of Bacteroides infection is currently unknown.

Only two species of Fusobacterium have been shown to produce extracellular enzymes (Table 3). The biologic importance of hyaluronidase and chondroitin sulfatase produced by F. mortiferum

TABLE 2. ENZYMES PRODUCED BY BACTEROIDES.

Bacteria	Enzyme	Reference
B. fragilis group	Heparinase	Steffen and Hentges[27] Gesner and Jenkin[28]
	Hyaluronidase Gelatinase Fibrinolysin Collagenase Superoxide dis- mutase	Steffen and Hentges[27] Rudek and Haque[29] Tally et al.[32]
B. melaninogenicus group	Phospholipase A Collagenase	Bulkacz et al.[30] Steffen and Hentges[27] Gibbons and Mac- Donald[31]
	Hyaluronidase Gelatinase Fibrinolysin	Steffen and Hentges[27] Rudek and Haque[29]

TABLE 3. ENZYMES PRODUCED BY
FUSOBACTERIUM.

Bacteria	Enzyme	Reference
F. mortiferum	Hyaluronidase Chondroitin sulfatase	Steffen and Hentges[27]
F. necrophorum	Phospholipase A Lysophospholipase	Abe et al.[36]

is unknown. Preliminary results from our laboratory suggest that phospholipase A and lysophospholipase produced by *F. necrophorum* may be responsible for the leukocidal and hemolytic activities which have been demonstrated in culture supernatants.

The capsular polysaccharide of *B. fragilis* has been implicated as an important factor in the virulence of this bacterium. Onderdonk et al. demonstrated that implantation of encapsulated *B. fragilis* in the peritoneal cavity of rats resulted in formation of abscesses.[37] Unencapsulated strains of Bacteroides produced abscesses only when implanted with facultative bacteria, i.e., enterococci. Formation of abscesses upon implantation of isolated capsular polysaccharide of *B. fragilis* was also documented. Immunization with the capsular polysaccharide protected against abscesses caused by intraperitoneal implantation of mixtures of enterococci and *B. fragilis* or *B. distasonis.*[38] Encapsulated *B. fragilis* has also been shown to adhere to rat peritoneal mesothelium,[39] an observation which may in part explain its abscess-forming capability.

It should be noted that there is controversy regarding the prevalence of encapsulation among species of the *B. fragilis* group. Kasper et al. observed capsules on strains of *B. fragilis* and reported that other species of the *B. fragilis* group were infrequently encapsulated.[40] Encapsulation was determined by electron microscopy of bacteria stained with ruthenium red, the wet mount India ink technique, and indirect immunofluorescence with antisera prepared against the capsular polysaccharide of *B. fragilis*. Using India ink staining, Babb and Cummins demonstrated encapsulation of strains of *B. fragilis, B. thetaiotaomicron, B. vulgatus,* and *B. ovatus,* but not *B. distasonis.*[41] We also have demonstrated surface polysaccharide on *B. thetaiotaomicron* by ruthenium red staining and electron microscopy,[42] and our recent results with additional isolates have confirmed the observation of Babb and Cummins. Thus, it is possible that the capsular polysaccharide of *B. fragilis* has unique properties which contribute to its greater virulence as compared with other species of the *B. fragilis* group.

Considerable attention has been focused on the biological activities of the lipopolysaccharide (LPS) moiety of the outer membrane complex (OMC) of Bacteroides and Fusobacterium. In marked contrast to the profound effects of LPS of facultative gram-negative bacilli on a number of host mediator systems, LPS of B. fragilis and B. melaninogenicus has been shown to have little or no endotoxic activity in the mouse or chick embryo lethality, limulus lysate, rabbit pyrogenicity, and dermal Schwartzman tests (Table 4). LPS of species of Fusobacterium has been shown to be more active than LPS of species of Bacteroides in these assays, but not as active as LPS of Salmonella enteritidis. Hofstad and Sveen have demonstrated that LPS of B. fragilis is chemotactic for polymorphonuclear leukocytes and that the chemotactic activity equaled that of LPS of F. nucleatum.[46] The difference in chemotactic activities between LPS of B. fragilis and S. enteritidis was far less pronounced than the difference in toxicity. The chemotactic activity appeared to be mediated by complement activation via the alternative pathway. The lack of endotoxic activity observed with LPS of the anaerobes

TABLE 4. COMPARISON OF BIOLOGICAL ACTIVITIES OF ISOLATED LIPOPOLYSACCHARIDES OF SALMONELLA, FUSOBACTERIUM, AND BACTEROIDES.

Assay	Representative concentration of LPS required for positive test (μg)*		
	Salmonella	Fusobacterium	Bacteroides
Lethality in actinomycin-D treated mice- (LD_{50})	0.2	2.0	26
Lethality in 11-day chick embryos- (LD_{50})	0.004	0.014	0.664
Gelation of limulus lysate	0.008	0.023	0.505
Pyrogenicity in rabbits -(FI_{40})	0.06	7.0	308.
Dermal Schwartzman reaction	5−25	10−50	>500

*References: Sveen et al.,[43] Kasper,[44] Mansheim et al.[45]

may explain why complications such as disseminated intravascular coagulation have been infrequently reported in patients with septicemia caused by members of the family Bacteroidaceae.[33]

The differences in biological activity observed with LPS of facultative and anaerobic gram-negative bacilli may be related to the chemical composition of the LPS molecules. LPS of facultative gram-negative bacilli has been shown to consist of a polysaccharide region covalently bound to a lipid region, termed lipid A.[47] The polysaccharide and lipid regions have been shown to be linked by a unique deoxysugar, 2-keto-3-deoxy-octonate (KDO), and heptose. Virtually all of the biologic activities associated with the LPS molecule have been shown to require the lipid A region; one exception is alternative pathway activation, in which an exclusive role for polysaccharide has been demonstrated.[47] Hofstad surveyed LPS of eight different Bacteroides species and nine different Fusobacterium species for the presence of heptose and KDO.[48] None of the LPS of the Bacteroides species was shown to contain detectable amounts of heptose or KDO; LPS of all Fusobacterium species was shown to contain small amounts of heptose and KDO. A typical lipid A moiety has been demonstrated in *Fusobacterium nucleatum*[49] but not Bacteroides.[44,45,50] These observations may explain the lack of biologic activity of LPS of Bacteroides and the intermediate biologic activity of LPS of Fusobacterium.

HOST DEFENSE MECHANISMS

Studies of the specificity of antibodies produced during Bacteroides infection have yielded conflicting information. In one investigation, cross-reactivity was demonstrated between antibodies to *B. fragilis* and *B. thetaiotaomicron* in the sera of patients with bacteremia or abscesses caused by these bacteria.[51] In other studies, cross-reactivity was generally not demonstrated between antibodies to different species of Bacteroides[52,53] or between antibodies directed against the same species.[54] The observed differences in specificity can probably be attributed to the use, in most of the studies, of crude antigen preparations containing multiple antigenic determinants and assays with varying degrees of sensitivity for the detection of antibodies.

Antigenic determinants with different specificities have been shown to reside in the OMC of Bacteroides. A species specific polysaccharide antigen has been isolated from the OMC of *B. fragilis* and *B. asaccharolyticus*, and it has been postulated that this antigen is capsular polysaccharide.[53,55-57] Protein in the OMC of B. fragilis has been shown to contain a species specific antigenic determinant.[55] LPS prepared by phenol-water extraction from B. fragilis and B. melaninogenicus has been shown to contain both species specific and strain specific antigenic determinants;[58,59] the demonstration of species specific antigenic determinants in the phenol-water extracts may reflect contamination with capsular polysaccharide.[45]

The contribution of humoral and cellular factors to the resistance against Bacteroides was first investigated by Casciato et al.[60] Utilizing an in vitro bactericidal assay, the interaction of pooled normal human serum and human polymorphonuclear leukocytes (PMNs) with fecal and clinical isolates of Bacteroides was determined under aerobic conditions. The fecal isolates were shown to be killed by sera alone, while killing of the clinical isolates required the combined action of sera and PMNs. Subsequent studies by these investigators demonstrated that certain clinical isolates of B. fragilis and B. thetaiotaomicron were susceptible to the bactericidal activity of normal human serum; the B. thetaiotaomicron strains were shown to be more susceptible than the B. fragilis strains.[61]

Utilizing a similar assay system, Bjornson et al. compared the in vitro interaction of pooled normal human serum and human PMNs with clinical isolates of B. fragilis and B. thetaiotaomicron under aerobic and anaerobic conditions.[62] In both environments, maximal killing of both Bacteroides strains required the combined action of PMNs and serum. Subsequent studies suggested that the normal human serum factors which facilitated opsonophagocytosis and intracellular killing of B. fragilis and B. thetaiotaomicron by human PMNs were immunoglobulin and components of the alternative complement pathway.[63] The antibodies in normal human serum which facilitate opsonophagocytosis and intracellular killing of Bacteroides were shown to belong to the IgM class and were directed against strain specific antigenic determinants contained in the OMC.[42,64]

The relative roles of immunoglobulin and the classical and alternative complement pathways in normal serum in facilitating opsonophagocytosis of Bacteroides by human PMNs were recently reported by Tofte et al.[65] Four strains of Bacteroides belonging to different species were used and opsonophagocytosis was measured by a radioassay. All of the strains were found to require immunoglobulin and classical and alternative pathway activity for optimal opsonophagocytosis. We have recently demonstrated heterogeneity in the requirements for classical and alternative pathway activity for opsonophagocytosis of 14 strains of the B. fragilis group belonging to different species with predominant utilization of the alternative pathway.

B. fragilis and *B. melaninogenicus* have been shown to reduce phagocytosis of *E. coli* by human PMNs in the presence of serum.[65] It was suggested that the Bacteroides strains were more efficiently opsonized than the *E. coli* strain and deprived the *E. coli* of sufficient opsonin. The ability of nine species of anaerobes to interfere with serum-mediated opsonophagocytosis and killing of *Proteus mirabilis* by human PMNs has also been reported.[66]

SUMMARY

Synergy between facultative and anaerobic bacteria in experimental infection has been well documented using various animal models. Production of hydrolytic enzymes and superoxide dismutase by gram-negative anaerobic bacilli has been demonstrated, however, the role of these enzymes in pathogenesis remains to be elucidated. LPS appears to play a minimal role in virulence presumably because of its unique structure. Capsular polysaccharide has been implicated as an important virulence factor of *B. fragilis*. Studies of host defense mechanisms operative in resistance against gram-negative anaerobic bacilli are in their infancy, but suggest that the in vitro interaction of human serum factors and PMNs with these bacteria is similar to that observed with facultative gram-negative bacilli.

REFERENCES

1. Finegold SM: Anaerobic Bacteria in Human Disease, Academic Press Inc. New York, 1977, pp. 26–34.
2. Finegold SM, Attebery HR, Sutter VL: Effect of diet on human fecal flora: Comparison of Japanese and American diets. Am J Clin Nutrit 27:1456–1469, 1974.
3. Bently DW, Nichols RL, Condon RE, Gorbach SL: The microflora of the human ileum and intraabdominal colon: Results of direct needle aspiration at surgery and evaluation of the technique. J Lab Clin Med 79:421–429, 1972.
4. Gorbach SL, Thadepalli H, Norsen J: Anaerobic microorganisms in intraabdominal infection. Anaerobic Bacteria: Role in Diesease. Balows A, DeHaan RM, Dowell VR Jr, Guze LB (eds.) Charles C. Thomas, Springfield, Ill, 1974, pp. 399–407.

5. Swenson RM, Lorber B, Michaelson TC, Spaulding EH: The bacteriology of intraabdominal infections. Arch Surg 109:398–399, 1974.
6. Brewer GE, Meleney FL: Progressive gangrenous infection of the skin and subcutaneous tissues, following operation for acute perforative appendicitis. Ann Surg 84:438–450, 1926.
7. Altemeier WA: The pathogenicity of the bacteria of appendicitis peritonitis. An experimental study. Surgery 11:374–384, 1942.
8. Hite KE, Locke M, Hesseltine HC: Synergism in experimental infections with nonsporulating anaerobic bacteria. J Infect Dis 84:1–9, 1949.
9. Rosebury T, Clark AR, Engel SG, Tergis F: Studies of fusospirochetal infection: I. Pathogenicity for guinea pigs of individual and combined cultures of spirochetes and other anaerobic bacteria derived from the human mouth. J Infect Dis 87:217–225, 1950.
10. Rosebury T, Clark AR, Tergis F, Engel SG: Studies of fusospirochetal infection: II. Analysis and attempted quantitative recombination of the flora of fusospirochetal infection after repeated guinea pig passage. J Infect Dis 87:226–233, 1950.
11. MacDonald JB, Sutton RM, Knoll ML: The production of fusospirochetal infections in guinea pigs with recombind pure cultures. J Infect Dis 95:275–284, 1954.
12. MacDonald JB, Sutton RM, Knoll ML, Madlener EM, Grainger RM: The pathogenic components of an experimental fusospirochetal infection. J Infect Dis 98:15–20, 1956.
13. MacDonald JB, Socransky SS, Gibbons RJ: Aspects of the pathogenesis of mixed anaerobic infections of mucous membranes. J Dent Res (Suppl) 42:529–544, 1963.
14. Socransky SS, Gibbons RJ: Required role of *Bacteroides melaninogenicus* in mixed anaerobic infections. J Infect Dis 115:247–253, 1965.
15. Hampp EG, Mergenhagen SE: Experimental intracutaneous fusobacterial and fusospirochetal infections. J Infect Dis 112:84–99, 1963.
16. Roberts DS: The pathogenic synergy of *Fusiformis necrophorus* and *Corynebacterium pyogenes:* I. Influence of the leukocidal exotoxin of *F. necrophorus*. Brit J Exp Path 48:665–673, 1967.
17. Roberts DS: The pathogenic synergy of *Fusiformis necrophorus* and *Corynebacterium pyogenes:* II. The response of *F. necrophorus* to a filtrable product of *C. pyogenes*. Brit J Exp Path 48:674–679, 1967.
18. Egerton JR, Roberts DS, Parsonson IM: The etiology and pathogenesis of ovine foot-rot: I. A histological study of the bacterial invasion. J Comp Path 79:207–216, 1969.
19. Roberts DS, Egerton JR: The etiology and pathogenesis of ovine foot-rot: II. The pathogenic association of *Fusiformis nodosus* and *F. necrophorus*. J Comp Path 79:217–227, 1969.
20. Weinstein WM, Onderdonk AB, Bartlett JG, Gorbach SL: Experimental intraabdominal abscesses in rats: Development of an experimental model. Infect Immun 10:1250–1255, 1974.

21. Onderdonk AB, Bartlett JG, Louie T, Sullivan-Seigler N, Gorbach SL: Microbial synergy in experimental intraabdominal abscess. Infect Immun 13:22–26, 1976.
22. Lykkegaard Nielsen M, Asnaes S, Justesen T: Susceptibility of the liver and biliary tract to anaerobic infection in extrahepatic biliary tract obstruction: III. Possible synergistic effect between anaerobic and aerobic bacteria. An experimental study in rabbits. Scand J Gastroent 11:263–272, 1976.
23. Kelly MJ: The quantitative and histologic demonstration of pathogenic synergy between *Escherichia coli* and *Bacteroides fragilis* in guinea pig wounds. J Med Microbiol 11:513–523, 1978.
24. Olsson B, Nord C, Wadstrom T: Formation of β-lactamase in *Bacteroides fragilis:* Cell-bound and extracellular activity. Antimicrob Agents Chemother 9:727–735, 1976.
25. Weinrich AE, Del Bene VE: Beta-lactamase activity in anaerobic bacteria. Antimicrob Agents Chemother 10:106–111, 1976.
26. O'Keefe JP, Tally FP, Barza M, Gorbach SL: Inactivation of penicillin G during experimental infection with *Bacteroides fragilis*. J Infect Dis 137:437–442, 1978.
27. Steffen EK, Hentges DJ: Hydrolytic enzymes of anaerobic bacteria isolated from human infections. J Clin Microbiol 14:153–156, 1981.
28. Gesner BM, Jenkin CR: Production of heparinase by bacteroides. J Bacteriol 81:595–604, 1961.
29. Rudek W, Haque R: Extracellular enzymes of the genus Bacteroides. J Clin Microbiol 4:458–460, 1976.
30. Bulkacz J, Erbland JF, MacGregor J: Phospholipase A activity in supernatants from cultures of *Bacteroides melaninogenicus*. Biochim Biophys Acta 664:148–155, 1981.
31. Gibbons RJ, MacDonald JB: Degradation of collagenous substrates by *Bacteroides melaninogenicus*. J Bacteriol 81:614–621, 1961.
32. Tally FP, Goldin BR, Jacobus NV, Gorbach SL: Superoxide dismutase in anaerobic bacteria of clinical significance. Infect Immun 16:20–25, 1977.
33. Chow AW, Guze LB: *Bacteroidaceae* bacteremia: Clinical experience with 112 patients. Medicine 53:93–126, 1974.
34. Felner JM, Dowell VR Jr: "Bacteroides" bacteremia. Am J Med 50:787–796, 1971.
35. Newman MG: The role of *Bacteroides melaninogenicus* and other anaerobes in peridontal infections. Rev Infect Dis 1:313–323, 1979.
36. Abe PM, Kendall CJ, Stauffer LR, Holland JW: Hemolytic activity of *Fusobacterium necorphorum* culture supernatants due to presence of phospholipase A and lysophospholipase. Am J Vet Res 40:92–96, 1979.
37. Onderdonk AB, Kasper DL, Cisneros RL, Bartlett JG: The capsular polysaccharide of *Bacteroides fragilis* as a virulence factor: Comparison of the pathogenic potential of encapsulated and unencapsulated strains. J Infect Dis 136:82–89, 1977.
38. Kasper DL, Onderdonk AB, Crabb J, Bartlett JG: Protective efficacy of

immunization with capsular antigen against experimental infection with *Bacteroides fragilis.* J Infect Dis 140:724–731, 1979.

39. Onderdonk AB, Moon NE, Kasper DL, Bartlett JG: Adherence of *Bacteroides fragilis* in vivo. Infect Immun 19:1083–1087, 1978.
40. Kasper DL, Hayes ME, Reinap BG, Craft FO, Onderdonk AB, Polk BF: Isolation and identification of encapsulated strains of *Bacteroides fragilis.* J Infect Dis 136:75–81, 1977.
41. Babb JL, Cummins CS: Encapsulation of Bacteroides species. Infect Immun 19:1088–1091, 1978.
42. Bjornson AB, Bjornson HS, Kitko BP: Specificity of immunoglobulin M antibodies in normal human serum that participate in opsonophagocytosis and intracellular killing of *Bacteroides fragilis* and *Bacteroides thetaiotaomicron* by human polymorphonuclear leukocytes. Infect Immun 30:263–271, 1980.
43. Sveen K, Hofstad T, Milner KC: Lethality for mice and chick embryos, pyrogenicity in rabbits and ability to gelate lysate from amoebocytes of *Limulus polyphemus* by lipopolysaccharides from *Bacteroides Fusobacterium,* and *Veillonella.* Acta Path Microbiol Scand Sect B 85:388–396, 1977.
44. Kasper DL: Chemical and biological characterization of the lipopolysaccharide of *Bacteroides fragilis* subspecies *fragilis.* J Infect Dis 134:59–66, 1976.
45. Mansheim BJ, Onderdonk AB, Kasper DL: Immunochemical and biological studies of the lipopolysaccharide of *Bacteroides melaninogenicus* subspecies *asaccharolyticus.* J. Immunol 120:72–78, 1978.
46. Hofstad T, Sveen K: The chemotactic effect of *Bacteroides fragilis* lipopolysaccharide. Rev Infect Dis 1:342–346, 1979.
47. Morrison DC, Ulevitch RJ: The effects of bacterial endotoxins on host mediation systems. Am J Pathol 93:527–617, 1978.
48. Hofstad T: The distribution of heptose and 2-keto-3-deoxy-octonate in *Bacteroidaceae.* J Gen Microbiol 85:314–320, 1974.
49. Hase S, Hofstad T, Rietschel ET: Chemical structure of the lipid A component of lipopolysaccharide from *Fusobacterium nucleatum.* J Bacteriol 129:9–14, 1977.
50. Mansheim BJ, Onderdonk AB, Kasper DL: Immunochemical characterization of surface antigens of *Bacteroides melaninogenicus.* Rev Infect Dis 1:263–275, 1979.
51. Rissing JP, Buxton TB, Edmundson HT: Detection of specific IgG antibody in sera from patients infected with *Bacteroides fragilis* by enzyme-linked immunosorbent assay. J Infect Dis 140:994–998, 1979.
52. Lambe DW, Danielsson D, Vroon DH, Carver RK: Immune response in eight patients infected with *Bacteroides fragilis.* J Infect Dis 131:499–508, 1975.
53. Mansheim BJ, Kasper DL: Detection of anticapsular antibodies to *Bacteroides asaccharolyticus* in serum from rabbits and humans by use of an enzyme-linked immunosorbent assay. J Infect Dis 140:945–951, 1979.

54. Danielsson D, Lambe DW, Persson S: The immune response in a patient to an infection with *Bacteroides fragilis* ss *fragilis* and *Clostridium difficile*. Acta Path Microbiol Scand Sect B 80:709–712, 1972.

55. Kasper DL, Seiler MW: Immunochemical characterization of the outer membrane complex of *Bacteroides fragilis* subspecies *fragilis*. J Infect Dis 132:440–450, 1975.

56. Mansheim BJ, Kasper DL: Purification and immunochemical characterization of the outer membrane of *Bacteroides melaninogenicus* subspecies *asaccharolyticus*. J Infect Dis 135:787–799, 1977.

57. Mansheim BJ, Solstad C, Kasper D: Identification of a subspecies-specific capsular antigen from *Bacteroides melaninogenicus* subspecies *asaccharolyticus* by immunofluorescence and electron microscopy. J Infect Dis 138:736–741, 1978.

58. Hofstad T: Serological properties of lipopolysaccharide from oral strains of *Bacteroides melaninogenicus*. J Bacteriol 97:1078–1082, 1969.

59. Hofstad T: O-antigenic specificity of lipopolysaccharides from *Bacteroides fragilis* ss *fragilis*. Acta Path Microbiol Scand Sect B 83:477–481, 1975.

60. Casciato DA, Rosenblatt JE, Goldberg LS, Bluestone R: In vitro interaction of *Bacteroides fragilis* with polymorphonuclear leukocytes and serum factors. Infect Immun 11:337–342, 1975.

61. Casciato DA, Rosenblatt JE, Bluestone R, Goldberg LS, Finegold SM: Susceptibility of isolates of Bacteroides to the bactericidal activity of normal human serum. J Infect Dis 140:109–113, 1979.

62. Bjornson AB, Altemeier WA, Bjornson HS: Comparison of the in vitro bactericidal activity of human serum and leukocytes against *Bacteroides fragilis* and *Fusobacterium mortiferum* in aerobic and anaerobic environments. Infect Immun 14:843–847, 1976.

63. Bjornson AB, Bjornson HS: Participation of immunoglobulin and the alternative complement pathway in opsonization of *Bacteroides fragilis* and *Bacteroides thetaiotaomicron*. J Infect Dis 138:351–358, 1978.

64. Bjornson AB, Bjornson HS, Kitko BP: Participation of normal human immunoglobulins M, G, and A in opsonophagocytosis and intracellular killing of *Bacteroides fragilis* and *Bacteroides thetaiotaomicron* by human polymorphonuclear leukocytes. Infect Immun 28:633–637, 1980.

65. Tofte RT, Peterson PK, Schmeling D, Bracke J, Kim Y, Quie PG: Opsonization of four Bacteroides species: Role of the classical complement pathway and immunoglobulin. Infect Immun 27:784–792, 1980.

66. Ingham HR, Sisson PR, Tharagonnet D, Seldon JB, Codd AA: Inhibition of phagocytosis in vitro by obligate anaerobes. Lancet II:1252–1254, 1977.

CHAPTER FIVE

Recurrent Sepsis

H. Harlan Stone, M.D.

Recurrent sepsis is a ubiquitous problem that is often un-
derrepresented in statistical reviews of infection rate. This is not
surprising, perhaps since in many cases the patient has already
gone home before recurrence is noted and thus any subsequent
abscess either discharges spontaneously or is drained in the outpa-
tient department. Accordingly, such instances of recurrent infection
rarely appear on the surgical record at the time of hospital review.

Three interacting factors are responsible for the development of
any surgical infection: inoculum itself; nutrition available to the
contaminating bacteria, such as blood clot; and host resistance.
Each is also involved in recurrent sepsis; but the inoculum, particularly its anaerobic component, is probably the most important of the
three in this regard.

ROLE OF COLON PERFORATION

Follow-up of patients who have developed sepsis after abdominal
surgery for penetrating wounds and for appendicitis reveal a significant correlation of such infection with appendiceal and colon perfo-

ration.[1] Patients with penetrating wounds that have not penetrated the colon, early appendicitis, or a perforated duodenal ulcer have a subsequent peritoneal sepsis rate of about 2% (Table 1).[1] Subsequent to colon perforation or more advanced appendicitis, both essentially with large bowel content spill into the peritoneal cavity, the rate for recurrent intraabdominal infection rises to 8% or greater (Table 2).[1]

TABLE 1. INTRAABDOMINAL INFECTION AFTER EMERGENCY CELIOTOMY—INCIDENCE IN CLEAN CASES.[1]

	Number	Infected	%
Perf. Duo. Ulcer	29	1	3
Enterolysis	54	0	0
Simple Appendicitis	73	0	0
Sup. Appendicitis	41	1	2
Gastric Perforation	72	2	3
Duodenal Perforation	31	1	3
Small Bowel Perforation	150	3	2
Trauma Without GI Perforation	362	8	2
Miscellaneous Peritonitis	32	2	6
Total	844	18	2.1

TABLE 2. INTRAABDOMINAL INFECTION AFTER EMERGENCY CELIOTOMY—INCIDENCE IN CONTAMINATED CASES.[1]

	Number	Infected	%
Perf. Gas. Ulcer	16	3	19
Enterostomy	36	2	6
Enterectomy	30	4	13
Colostomy	26	0	0
Gang. Appendicitis	36	5	14
Perf. Appendicitis	94	9	10
Colostomy Closure	71	0	0
Colon Perforation	126	14	11
Rectal Perforation	9	1	11
Total	444	38	8.6

**TABLE 3. WOUND INFECTION AFTER
PRIMARY CLOSURE—INCIDENCE LESS
THAN 10%.**[1]

	Number	Infected	%
Perf. Duo. Ulcer	13	1	8
Enterolysis	47	1	2
Simple Appendicitis	71	1	1
Sup. Appendicitis	31	2	6
Gastric Perforation	35	3	9
Duodenal Perforation	8	0	0
Small Bowel Perforation	56	5	9
Trauma without GI Perfo- ration	283	8	3
Miscellaneous Peritonitis	23	2	9
Total	567	23	4.1

**TABLE 4. WOUND INFECTION AFTER
PRIMARY CLOSURE—INCIDENCE MORE
THAN 10%.**[1]

	Number	Infected	%
Perf. Gas. Ulcer	9	2	22
Enterostomy	14	7	50
Enterectomy	9	5	56
Colostomy	6	1	17
Gang. Appendicitis	12	6	50
Perf. Appendicitis	25	16	64
Colostomy Closure	23	4	17
Colcn Perforation	52	33	63
Rectal Perforation	4	1	25
Total	154	75	48.7

The difference between the two groups with respect to incidence of infection in the surgical incision is even more striking.[1] After operations for early appendicitis or for surgical management of abdominal trauma without large bowel perforation, the surgical wound infection rate is only 4% (Table 3.)[1] However, when colon contents have spilled, as in advanced appendicitis or when the colon itself has been perforated, wound infection rates reach almost 50% when primary closure of the skin and subcutaneous tissue is done (Table 4).[1]

GROWING THE ANAEROBES

It is not only possible to correlate certain disease processes with recurrent sepsis, but also specific groups of bacteria with such as well. However, proper culture technique and strict attention to anaerobe isolation and identification are explicitly required. A simple swab will seldom grow out any anaerobe other than *Bacteroides fragilis*. Resultant isolates will be primarily aerobic. By contrast, anaerobes can be grown in fairly large numbers if properly secured aspirates of frank pus or contaminated fluid are immediately and appropriately processed.[2]

The peritoneal cavity should be aspirated immediately on opening the abdomen or just before the peritoneum is entered. Aspiration must be performed quickly and with minimal exposure of the aspirate to atmospheric oxygen, inasmuch as anaerobes vary considerably in their susceptibility to the lethal effects of oxygen. The most virulent species may die before a pus sample can be placed under anaerobic conditions, thereby producing culture results that in no way reflect the true microbial components of the infection.

The most efficient method is aspiration with a large bore needle and syringe. After collection, the needle can be stuck into a rubber stopper and the syringe used as the transport vehicle. The specimen should then be inoculated immediately into prereduced media under anaerobic conditions. Finally, immediate incubation at 37C is crucial, since cold retards the cellular metabolism of some major anaerobes, thus permitting overgrowth by other, possibly less virulent, organisms. When collected and cultured properly, aspirates from patients with a large bowel perforation almost routinely show aerobic organisms, averaging about two species per subject. In almost all of these patients, two or more species of anaerobe can be grown from the specimen as well.[3]

CLUES FROM INFECTION SITE AND STAGE

Laboratory assessments take time however, so it is almost always necessary to make empiric decisions regarding treatment before the culture report is available. Careful bacteriologic survey has demonstrated that sepsis associated with large bowel perforations is due to a polymicrobial mix of aerobes with anaerobes, while small bowel perforations produce primarily an aerobic peritonitis.[2] In other words, site of origin of the contaminant uniformly determines which

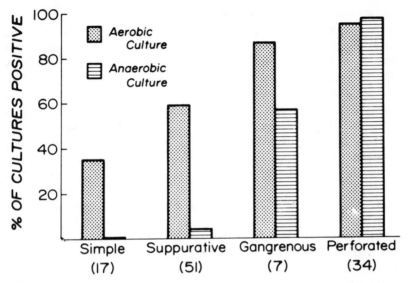

FIG. 1. Relative incidence of aerobic and anaerobic contaminating the peritoneal cavity of patients with appendicitis.[2]

species, or combinations of bacteria, will reach the peritoneal cavity to initiate the anticipated subsequent infection.

The stage of infection is also important. Appendicitis offers a good example (Figure 1).[2] Early appendicitis (i.e., simple or suppurative) is usually an aerobic infection. Anaerobes are very rarely present until gangrenous changes occur in the appendiceal wall. Once gangrene has set in, however, with or without gross perforation, anaerobes join the polymicrobial flora and soon become dominant. This conversion of a primarily aerobic set of organisms to a mixture of aerobic and anaerobic flora holds true in most instances of mechanical small bowel obstruction; whenever intestinal contents become stagnant, anaerobic bacteria uniformly overgrow the initially more dominant aerobic species.[2]

THERAPY: AGGRESSIVE AND ANTIANAEROBIC

Anaerobes are known to elaborate extracellular and membrane-associated enzymes that increase pathogen virulence against host tissue and host defenses. Examples of such have been the increased severity and increased incidence of bacteremia whenever proteolytic enzymes (e.g., Varidase or Travase) are purposely introduced into the area of infection. In many cases, the patient contributes his own similar enzymes, as with a pancreatic abscess. Otherwise, the detrimental enzyme is provided by anaerobic species participating in the polymicrobial pathogen population.[2]

Treatment of the recurrent infection is specifically designed to eliminate the action of such proteolytic enzymes and is based on two very simple, but effective, procedures. First, and most important, is the excision of all necrotic tissue as well as the conversion of the infectious process into an open wound. Anaerobes can exist and propagate only when the local oxidation-reduction potential has been significantly reduced. Exposure to atmospheric concentrations of oxygen significantly increases this redox potential.[2] Secondly, an agent with specific activity against the anticipated anaerobic species should be administered.[3]

Delayed primary closure (i.e., leaving the superficial portion of the incision open to provide for exposure to atmospheric oxygen) is an effective approach that has been well-documented.[1] Aggressive removal of all purulent material and necrotic tissue is crucial to successful therapy.[2] Antimicrobial agents cannot substitute for a timid surgeon or negligence in basic wound care.

IDENTIFYING THE RECURRENCE

Intraabdominal abscesses tend to occur: (1) in the true pelvis; (2) in the gutters on either side of the pelvis, communicating with one another by way of the false pelvis; and (3) in the subphrenic spaces.

Pelvic abscesses are relatively easy to diagnose by rectal and/or pelvic examination and are best drained through a transrectal approach. Before the drain is inserted however, it is wise to make certain that the palpable mass is indeed an abscess, not a loop of bowel or the distended bladder. Needle aspiration of about one ml of material will make this important differentiation and provide a sample for scientific culture as well. Aspiration of more than one ml should be avoided, for it will cause collapse of the abscess cavity and thus loss of the original palpable mass. After the initial aspiration, an Adson or Kelly clamp is pushed transrectally into the abscess; this is followed by insertion of a Malecot catheter, which then comes out the rectum. The catheter is connected to a straight drainage system (i.e., urine drainage tube and bag) and is taped to an adjacent thigh to prevent dislodgement). Within two or three days after the procedure, the stretched anal sphincter regains its tone, so it is best to remove the catheter in order to avoid unnecessary patient discomfort.

The usual *midabdominal abscess* presents as a spontaneously-discharging subfascial infection. Abscess formation within the *subphrenic space* is somewhat more difficult to identify. If anaerobes are involved, the gases they produce are absorbed slowly and thus tell-tale bubbles will appear on an over-penetrated thoracoabdominal x-ray. The question as to whether such gas is extraluminal or intraluminal can generally be resolved by a contrast study. Aerobes produce carbon dioxide, as a principle product of metabolism, which so rapidly diffuses and is so readily absorbed that an identifying collection of gas seldom is found. Because of this absence of bubbles, the CAT scan has become the most useful clinical tool for identifying the subphrenic abscess.

Diagnosis by gallium-67 scanning has not lived up to its original promise. The abscess to blood ratios of 8:1 is not sufficiently greater than what is noted in a healing wound. Results can thus be quite confusing. Accordingly, the CAT scan still remains the most reliable method despite many other new tests based upon the labelling of neutrophils with other radioactive substances.

Both midabdominal and subphrenic abscesses are drained through an abdominal incision. Transverse placement of the incision generally provides more reliable drainage. Both abscess foci also demand dependent drainage (transrectal drainage of pelvic infections assures dependence), so that the patient should ideally be placed prone. If this is impossible, a sump drain should be used to overcome the effect of gravity.

PREVENTION OF RECURRENCE

The greatest threat to patient survival has been shown to be a bacteremia due to gram-negative rods, most frequently *E. coli*. Patients die of endotoxemia. Bacteroides bacteremia is seldom, if ever, lethal, but patients with a Bacteroides infection almost always have a gram-negative rod present as well. Accordingly, antibiotic coverage must be directed primarily against this gram-negative rod, which carries by far the greater mortality rate.

In considering antibiotic prophylaxis against anaerobic bacteremia, the clinical review by Fry et al. is of particular interest.[4] Patients with Bacteroides bacteremia who were given a specific antianaerobic agent had a mortality rate of 44%. Among those given a drug known to be ineffective against the anaerobe, mortality was only 38%. It would seem therefore that the patients receiving the wrong drug were better off, but this of course was not a truly statistically significant difference. What it did show, however, was that administration of antibiotics with proven activity against the anaerobe cannot be correlated with an improved mortality rate.

A study of recurrent infections performed at Emory gave similar findings.[5] If cefotaxime was effective against the aerobic organisms, the cure rate was 85%. If the organisms were resistant to cefotaxime, however, the cure rate was only 56%. The same was true when gentamicin plus clindamycin was administered: an 83% cure rate if aerobic pathogens were susceptible contrasted to 55% when the aerobes were resistant. As far as the anaerobic species participating in the infection were concerned, the cure rate remained the same (i.e., 82% to 88%) regardless of whether or not the antibiotic used was effective or ineffective against these specific pathogens.

Such findings suggest that the importance of anaerobes participating in polymicrobial sepsis is due primarily to their role in facilitating recurrent infection, not in their isolated contribution to mortality. In other words, antibiotic therapy directed specifically against the anaerobe can significantly reduce the incidence of recurrent infection. This has been clearly shown in a randomized trial of gentamicin plus clindamycin versus gentamicin plus metronidazole (Table 5).[6] Patients given metronidazole had a much lower incidence of recurrent sepsis than did those receiving clindamycin (i.e., 3% versus 19%). Although no differences in antianaerobic efficacy could be noted by in vitro testing of these two agents, their pharmacokinetic properties do appear to differ considerably. In particular, the longer half-life of metronidazole and its

TABLE 5. EFFECTIVENESS OF TWO-DRUG COMBINATION IN PREVENTING RECURRENT SEPSIS (p=<0.05).[6]

Drug combination	No. of patients treated for sepsis	No. in whom sepsis recurred	Recurrence rate
Gentamicin-clindamycin	68	13	19%
Gentamicin-metronidazole	60	2	3%

better tissue distribution provide more reliable and prolonged penetration into deeply infected areas.[7]

Regardless of the antibiotic used, however, circumstances that limit excellent capillary perfusion and thus inhibit tissue penetration by the antimicrobial agent also invite recurrent sepsis. Patients in shock and those whose wounds involve subcutaneous fat are especially at risk for this very reason. The characteristically poor blood supply of subcutaneous fat almost guarantees inadequate antibiotic delivery to the injured tissue unless high blood levels are maintained for an extended period of time. It is for this same reason that such tissues have relatively low concentrations of the host's own humoral defense factors. Thus, closure of infected wounds with flaps composed only of skin or subcutaneous tissue usually results in a recurrent infection and commonly a slough of the entire flap in contrast to the almost uniform success gained by use of a flap based on healthy muscle, the myocutaneous flap.

SUMMARY

Anaerobes play a major role in recurrent sepsis. At present, their influence on overall mortality is moot. Consequently, the prevention of recurrence should include measures specifically directed against anaerobic organisms—aggressive debridement of all necrotic tissue, selective wound closure, appropriate dependent drainage, and effective antibiotic therapy of the aerobic as well as the anaerobic component.

REFERENCES

1. Stone HH, Hester Jr TR: Incisional and peritoneal infection after emergency celiotomy. Annals of Surgery 177:669, 1973.
2. Stone HH, et al.: Incidence and significance of intraperitoneal anaerobic bacteria. Annals of Surgery 181:705, 1981.
3. Bartlett JG, et al.: A review, lessons from an animal model of intraabdominal sepsis. Archives of Surgery 113:853, 1978.
4. Fry DE, et al.: Clinical implications in Bacteroides bacteremia. Surgery, Gynecology & Obstetrics 149:189, 1979.
5. Stone HH, et al.: Clinical comparison of cefotaxime versus the combination of gentamicin plus clindamycin in the treatment of peritonitis and similar polymicrobial soft tissue surgical sepsis. Clinical Therapeutics 4 (suppl A):67–80, 1981.

6. Stone HH, Fabian TC: Clinical comparison of antibiotic combinations in the treatment of peritonitis and related mixed aerobic-anaerobic surgical sepsis. World Journal of Surgery 4:415, 1980.
7. Templeton R: Metabolism and pharmacokinetics of metronidazole; a review. Proceedings of the International Metronidazole Conference (Montreal, 1976). Excerpta Medica (1977), pp. 28–49.

CHAPTER SIX

Anastomotic Failure

Thomas K. Hunt, M.D.

Colonic and rectal anastomoses are more subject to leakage than anastomoses in other parts of the gastrointestinal tract. In 1970, colonic anastomotic leaks were reported in several series to have occurred in 2 to 15% of patients undergoing colectomy, with 8 to 48% wound infections and 14 to 60% total bacterial complications. Over the subsequent 12 years, the average figures have dropped to about 5 to 10% colonic leaks, with an average of 4 to 15% wound infections. In my opinion, the major impact on the 1970 statistics has been the result of two clinical advances: increased sophistication in the use of antibiotics for surgical prophylaxis, and improved resuscitation and anesthesia techniques that maintain good tissue perfusion, nutrition, and oxygenation. Both can be exploited to even greater advantage in the never ending battle against infection.

THE ROLE OF INFECTION

The fact that the number of anastomotic failures is decreasing at about the same rate as the number of peritoneal infections leads to an important question: Is it possible that the infection is as much a cause of the anastomotic leak as the leak is the cause of the infection?

Over the years, reports from both surgeons and pathologists have noted that many so-called anastomotic leaks are near but not *at* the anastomotic line. Based on this ubiquitous finding, Hawley et al.[1] and Irvin et al.[2-5] devised a set of experiments to test, among other objects, the hypothesis that the leak was as much the result of the infection as the cause of it.

Colon anastomoses were performed in rabbits, followed in some animals by intraperitoneal application of sterile autoclaved stool with one ml of *E. coli* and *S. faecalis* in a mixed culture of 10% bacteria. A far greater number of leaks were found in the animals given peritoneal infection. Infected anastomoses showed a statistically significant reduction in bursting pressure at seven days compared with normal controls. Bursting strength of an anastomosis is normally reduced in the first two postoperative days and then rises. In the animals with peritonitis, however, tensile strength continued to fall until either abscess formation or free perforation became inevitable. Certainly peritonitis tends to cause "anastomotic leaks," but there are other mechanisms by which leaks can occur first.

COLLAGEN SYNTHESIS AND LYSIS

In 1968, Cronin, Jackson, and Dunphy[6] introduced the concept that wound healing is a struggle between the lysis and synthesis of collagen. Normal collagen is rapidly lysed in all wounds. The strength of an anastomosis is the sum of the retained strength of the old collagen through which sutures are passed, plus that of the new collagen being synthesized by healing, minus the strength lost by lysis of the old collagen (Figure 1).[7] Thus, anything that impairs synthesis or increases lysis is likely to cause anastomotic failure. It follows that sutures in tissue whose instrinsic strength is diminished by lysis may not hold tissue together. Not surprisingly, Hawley et al. also found that the fall in tensile strength in infected rabbit anastomoses was associated with an equally significant decrease in collagen content of the colon around the anastomoses. At body temperature, pH, and ionic concentration, mature collagen is resistant to most proteolytic enzymes and is broken down only by the specific enzyme, collagenase, and certain lysosomal enzymes released by inflammatory leukocytes. After surgery in these infected animals, collagenase activity increased accounting for the increased breakdown of mature collagen.

The role of both local surgical trauma and remote trauma in

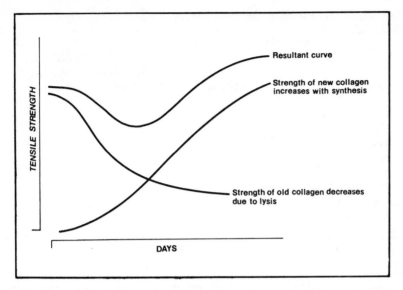

FIG. 1. Concept of wound strength expressed as a balance between lysis of the old collagen holding the sutures and of the new collagen welding the wound edges. Any deficit of synthesis or exaggeration of lysis makes the wound point weaker for a longer time. [7]

rupture of rat colon anastomoses was reported by Irvin and Hunt in 1974.[2,3] Local trauma consisted of a retroperitoneal dissection and biopsy of the psoas muscle; remote trauma was produced by a comminuted fracture of the femur.

Remote trauma had little effect on the tensile strength and collagen content of the anastomoses. Local trauma in the vicinity of the surgery, however, resulted in loss of colonic tensile strength and a leak rate of 26%.

The collagen content of the anastomoses in control animals subjected to no trauma was about 113 ng/mg dry tissue. Of the group subjected to intraabdominal trauma, those with intact anastomoses had significantly lower values, about 96 ng/mg. But in the animals with anastomotic rupture, collagen content went down to 88 ng/mg.

In a second study (Table 1),[2] the incidence of anastomotic dehiscence in one group of rats subjected to excessive intraabdominal trauma during colonic anastomoses was 19%. In animals subjected to identical trauma and anastomosis but who were also given interperitoneal cephalothin, however, dehiscence was only 3.6%. A third group of animals, given a diverting colostomy four weeks before colonic anastomosis, had no dehiscence. Thus, trauma predisposes to infection. Prevention of infection significantly reduces

TABLE 1. INCIDENCE OF ANASTOMOTIC DEHISCENCE. [2]

Group	No. of animals	Anastomotic dehiscence	Incidence of dehiscence (%)
Intraabdominal trauma	27	5*	18.5
Intraabdominal trauma and antibiotics	28	1	3.6
Intraabdominal trauma and colostomy	22	0	0

*Significantly higher incidence of dehiscence compared with the colostomy ($\chi^2 = 4.54$, P 0.05). "Antibiotics" = intraperitoneal cephalothin.

anastomotic disruption, and diverting colostomy prevents it altogether.

In normally healing primarily closed wounds, new collagen can be found as early as the second day, with the peak rate of synthesis occurring on the fifth to seventh day. In the process of collagen fiber formation, the submicroscopic soluble collagen molecules polymerize along their long axes with an overlap of approximately 25%. With the intermolecular crossbinding occurring mainly through covalent linkages between adjacent lysine molecules, the thick, strong collagen fibers are formed. These fibers, the major source of connective tissue strength, account for the return of tensile integrity to wound tissue. (Figure 2.).[7]

By about the third week, the primarily healing wound has reached its greatest mass. Thereafter, this mass of collagen and new vessels, perhaps a simplified counterpart of fracture callus, recedes, and the tissue softens while its collagen content diminishes and the new vessels regress. Paradoxically, the strength of the wound increases during this time. Behind the paradox lies the fact that by three weeks the fiber structure is being slowly remodeled into mechanically useful patterns to create a more effective structure with less collagen. Reorganization is not achieved merely by subtraction of collagen molecules; rather it involves replacement of the total collagenous mass. The gel-like collagen, which is deposited soon after injuries, is broken down into amino acids by the action of collagenase and lysosomal enzymes. These amino acids are resynthesized into colla-

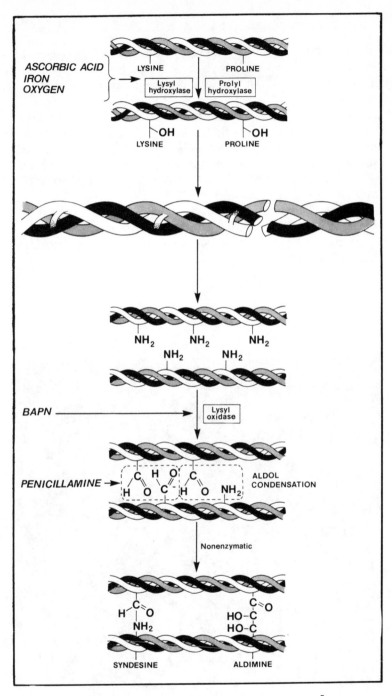

FIG. 2. Process of collagen fiber formation. [7]

gen right at the wound site. The closely packed gel-like character of the early wound gives way to an open "basket-weave" tissue structure (Figure 3).[7] The wound is repeatedly remodeled for six months to a year.

The details of collagenase activity are still controversial. The enzyme is produced by inflammatory cells, including polymorphonuclear leukocytes and macrophages. It is also produced by regenerating epidermis and by budding vascular endothelium. Its presence and its activity seem to be enhanced by steroids and inflammatory reactions.

Because collagen lysis is a destructive process, it demands less energy than the constructive process of synthesis. Thus lysis continues, indeed may even be accelerated, in the face of starvation or protein deficiency.

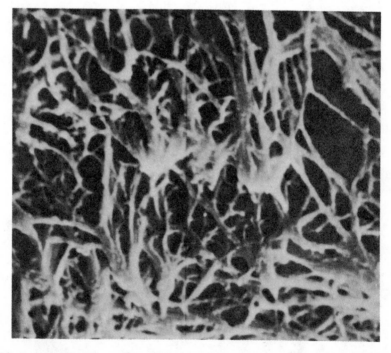

FIG. 3. Wound collagen at ten days by scanning electron microscopy. Note the lack of definition of collagen fibrils and the small fibers. Magnification X10,000. [7]

There is some evidence that in wounds, collagenase activity is particularly directed toward the already established, highly insoluble collagen. Several studies of rat colon, involving radioactive labelling of old collagen before wounding and new collagen after wounding, have shown old collagen to be preferentially destroyed. Thus tissue strength suffers until the new collagen can be adequately cross-linked.[4,5,8]

Removal of old collagen usually occurs only a few millimeters into normal tissue, of course. At this point, new collagen must interact with old to form a bond. The interaction may be an actual "weld," an interweaving of old and new fibers in a "darn," or both. Although it is difficult to find sharply cut collagen ends even in an early healing wound, electron microscopy reveals an interlacing of new and old fibers (Figure 4).

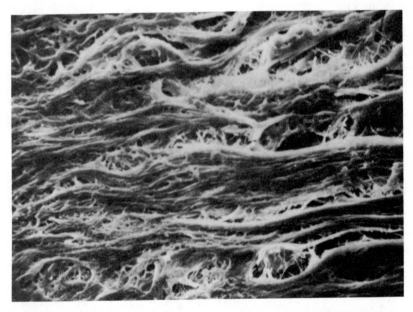

FIG. 4 Scanning electron microscopy of a healed wound. The old fibers are large and tapered and joined by the new less well organized scar collagen.

FACTORS AFFECTING COLLAGEN
METABOLISM

Obviously, the balance between lysis and synthesis is delicate; acceleration of lysis, deceleration of synthesis, or both, may make the difference between healing or no healing at all. And the surgeon preparing to perform a colonic anastomosis must be aware, in any given patient, of factors that decrease collagen synthesis or deposition and those that favor lysis (Table 2).

Of the factors that reduce synthesis, starvation is the most obvious. There is no doubt that a patient who has lost 15 to 20% of his or her body weight is at risk for anastomotic rupture. Protein deprivation has been shown to diminish collagen formation in wounds. Other more specific forms of starvation have also been

TABLE 2.[7]

Factors that decrease collagen synthesis
Preoperative
  Starvation (protein depletion)
  Steroids
  Infection (some types)
  Associated Injuries
  Hypoxia
  Radiation Injury
  Uremia
  Diabetes
  Advanced Age
Operative
  Tissue injury
  Poor blood supply
  Poor apposition of surrounding tissues (pelvic anastomosis)
Postoperative
  Starvation
  Hypovolemia
  Hypoxia
  Drugs—e.g., actinomycin, 5-FU, methotrexate, etc.
Factors that increase collagen lysis (all are active before and after operation)
  Starvation
  Severe Trauma
  Inflammation
  Infection
  Steroids

shown to interfere with collagen synthesis—ascorbic acid deficiency, or scurvy, for example, and lack of iron and zinc (Figure 5).[7]

Cortisone retards collagen synthesis and large doses delay the appearance of all components of healing. At one time it was thought that patients who continue to receive large amounts of cortisone postoperatively are particularly prone to anastomotic leaks. New information suggests that the effect of steroids on colon anastomosis is less than that seen in body wall wounds,[9] perhaps due to "growth hormones" in the gut.

Other factors are also well documented in the literature. Two should perhaps be emphasized here: hypovolemia and hypoxia, both of which have profound effects on wound healing and resistance to infection.

We do not consider a patient to be adequately perfused unless capillary return is less than one and one-half seconds after finger pressure is removed from his forehead, capillary return to the skin of his knees is less than five seconds, intraocular pressure is normal, his tongue is moist, he is not thirsty, and he is able to stand up without changes in vital signs lasting for more than a few seconds. Urine output is not a consideration—unless it is very low, of course—since it is not well associated with blood volume.

Even these rigid criteria do not always assure that wound perfusion is optimal, however. Using a device that measures wound extracellular fluid PO_2, we have found that even in patients thought to be well perfused, a little additional hydration, with 250 to 500 cc of saline, yields a significant increase in wound perfusion and oxygenation, an increase associated in theory, at least, with better healing and resistance to infection.[10-12]

In the 1970s, experimental and clinical evidence has shown hypoxia to be a fundamental characteristic of wounds. When tissue is disrupted, existing vessels are injured, some cells are damaged, and platelets and collagen intermingle and interact. Injured vessels thrombose as nearby vessels dilate. The injured tissue becomes overloaded with rapidly metabolizing white cells, which will soon be replaced by rapidly metabolizing fibroblasts—all this in an area of damaged vasculature. Thus, at the very time the injured tissue needs energy the most, its local circulation is least able to provide it. The result is a local hypoxia and lactic acidosis.[13]

This hypoxic environment probably accounts for the fact that surgical wound infections are predominantly anaerobic. One important bactericidal system, oxidative killing, uses oxygen selectively. After it ingests bacteria, the normal phagocyte increases its oxygen consumption as much as 20 times its basal rate. Some of the oxygen consumed in this respiratory burst is enzymatically reduced by a

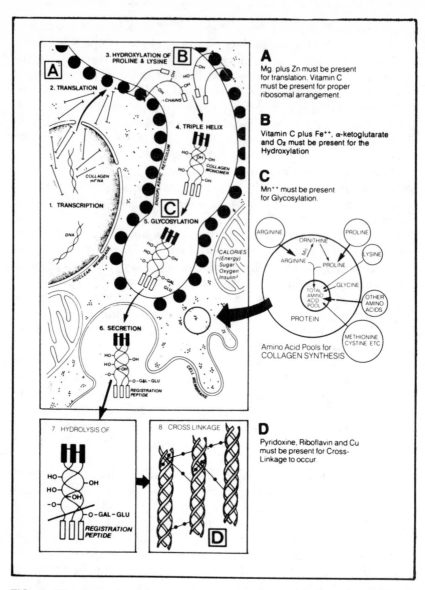

FIG. 5. Diagrammatic representation of steps in collagen synthesis, from translation to secretion, with their nutritional requirements. A proper mix of all nutrients is necessary for each step.[7]

single electron to form superoxide, an unstable molecule with bactericidal activity against certain strict anaerobes. Within the phagosome, superoxide is rapidly reduced to hydrogen peroxide, which also kills certain aerobic organisms. Other high-energy derivatives, such as hydroxyl radicals and singlet oxygen, formed during phagocytosis, may also be bactericidal.

Inhibition of the oxidative killing mechanism by the hypoxic environment of wounded tissue may account for the particular sensitivity of wounds to infection by a limited group of organisms. Without oxygen, superoxide cannot be made and leukocytes lose as much as half their killing power even aginst some aerobic organisms—S. aureus and E. coli in particular. Some anaerobes are killed by nonoxidative phagocytosis and degranulation. Unlike the aerobes, such organisms may not be protected by the lack of oxygen for oxidative killing. But in the oxygen deprived environment of the wound, their ability to proliferate and produce toxins is significantly increased.[14-18]

TECHNICAL CONSIDERATIONS

The decreasing leak rates seen in the 1970s probably have much more to do with increased knowledge of, and attention to, the metabolic factors discussed earlier than to any technical advancements. Still, the influence of surgical technique cannot be neglected.

The one technique at the surgeon's disposal that makes a difference between life and death is the diverting colostomy, which puts the anastomosis out of the fecal stream. Although the leak rate is not changed much by employing a proximal colostomy, mortality is greatly increased when such decompression is *not* performed in patients with obstructed, inflamed, or ischemic colon.

Beyond that decision, the most successful anastomosis is the one the individual surgeon does best, most accurately, gently, and, to some degree, most quickly. The surgeon must always keep in mind the major requirements for healing: excellent blood supply; absence of tension in suturing; watertight apposition of anastomotic edges; and gentle handling of tissues. Blood supply may be impaired by too many sutures, sutures tied too tightly, pressure from an intramural hematoma, or ligation of critical mesenteric vessels. Finally, the bowel's strongest layer, the submucosa, must be included in the principal layer of sutures.

A more specific requirement having to do with the all-important blood supply is for healthy tissue to surround the anastomosis. The high failure rate of pelvic anastomoses can be attributed in part to the simple anatomic fact that the pelvic colon is surrounded by a bony ring, so tissue cannot collapse around the repair and contribute blood supply to the healing process. One solution to that deficiency is to fashion an omental flap and bring it around the pelvic anastomosis to provide a parasitizable blood flow.

Staples are also particularly useful in low colon anastomoses that cannot be seen well enough to ensure accurate sewing. Nevertheless, technique is secondary to informed patient selection, appreciation of the criteria used to decide whether or not an anastomosis should be performed at all, and appropriate postoperative care.[19]

RISK FACTORS FOR ANASTOMOTIC FAILURE

When considering whether or not to do an anastomosis, surgeons must look at all adverse factors affecting anastomotic healing. A 1973 survey by Schrock et al. of 1700 colon anastomoses performed at the University of California revealed a mean leak rate of 4.5%. Only 1.7% occurred in younger patients without a number of adverse factors identified in the study. However, a 6.7% leak rate occurred in patients with at least one of the risk factors (Tables 3, 4, and 5).[9]

Advanced age was found to put patients at risk. Age is a wound healing factor probably related to cardiopulmonary function. "Anemia" was a danger sign, but I think it was probably related more to conditions often associated with anemia, such as malnutrition, abnormalities of circulating blood volume, and increased blood

TABLE 3. SINGLE VARIABLES. [9]

Variable	Category	Anastomoses	Leaks	P
Age (Years)	0–10	57	3 (5.3%)	$p > 0.25$
	11–40	230	5 (2.2%)	—
	41–60	642	24 (3.7%)	$p > 0.25$
	61–80	720	39 (5.4%)	$p < 0.05$
	81+	52	5 (9.6%)	$p < 0.01$
Anemia	>35	370	26 (7.0%)	$p < 0.025$
(Hematocrit)	<35	1281	48 (3.7%)	
Radiation	Yes	35	5 (14.3%)	$p < 0.01$
Therapy	No	786	36 (4.6%)	

TABLE 4. SINGLE VARIABLES. [9]

Variable	Category	Anastomoses	Leaks	P
Schedule	Elective	1505	61 (4.1%)	$p < 0.025$
	Emergency	195	16 (8.2%)	
Infection	Yes	200	21 (10.5%)	$p < 0.005$
	No	1503	56 (3.7%)	
Intraoperative	Yes	84	9 (10.7%)	$p < 0.01$
Hypotension	No	1507	66 (4.4%)	
Intraoperative	0.1	1259	41 (3.3%)	
Transfusions	2.3	261	22 (8.4%)	$p < .001$
(Units)	4 or more	74	12 (16.2%)	$p > 0.05$
Duration of	<3	440	14 (3.2%)	
Operation	3.5	823	33 (4.0%)	
(Hours)	>5	323	28 (8.7%)	$p < 0.01$

TABLE 5. SINGLE VARIABLES. [9]

Variable	Category	Anastomoses	Leaks	P
Peritoneal				
Level	Intraperitoneal	1411	48 (3.4%)	$p < 0.005$
	Extraperitoneal	251	26 (10.4%)	
Segment	SB to right colon	577	22 (3.8%)	
	Colocolic	579	19 (3.3%)	
	Left colocolic	408	13 (3.2%)	
	Left colorectal	368	34 (9.2%)	$p < 0.005$
Carcinoma at				
Margins	Yes	15	3 (20.0%)	$p < 0.01$
	No	542	23 (4.2%)	

viscosity than to the anemia itself. Mild or moderate, uncomplicated, normovolemic anemia in otherwise healthy animals does not impair delivery of oxygen to the wound and is of no consequence in wound healing.[20]

Past radiation was a major problem, which raised the rupture rate by a factor of nearly four. The danger of leakage attributable to radiation is generally proportional to the degree of visible radiation damage. If the bowel feels and looks normal, it will heal normally; but if it looks like a radiated bowel, and if it feels stiff and ischemic, successful anastomosis may be impossible.

Intraoperative transfusion was also associated with leak rate. Transfusion does not burst anastomoses, of course. The association has to do with the degree of trauma of surgery.

When infection and severe inflammation were present at the time of the original operation, the leak rate increased in the small bowel and right colon by a factor of two, in the left colon by a factor of six, and in the colorectal area by a factor of about three.

Anastomoses in the stomach and small bowel are usually performed even in the presence of suboptimal systemic conditions. Often there are no satisfactory alternatives, and these repairs usually heal well anyway. So a perforated gastric ulcer may be treated by subtotal gastrectomy despite the presence of early peritonitis. Colonic anastomoses do not heal as reliably, however. Thus, when adverse factors are present and the surgeon must decide whether or not to do an anastomosis, he must weigh the adverse factors against the alternative of doing a colostomy or resecting the involved bowel and leaving anastomosis for another time.

Severe trauma with associated blood loss represents two marks against immediate anastomosis, for example. Recent shock would be a third, uremia a fourth. Mild diabetes is not a problem, but a patient who is out of control and hyperglycemic gets a definite mark against anastomosis. Once the score reaches 4+ as roughly suggested in Table 6, the wiser decision often is to wait.[21]

ANTIMICROBIAL MEASURES

The evidence cited earlier in this paper, as well as numerous other studies, amply demonstrate that colonic resection with primary anastomosis is a procedure that places the patient at high risk of postoperative infection. Inasmuch as infection at, or near, the anastomosis is a major risk factor for leakage, the elimination of potentially infective microorganisms is not only justified but mandatory when a colon anastomosis is to be performed. Adequate preparation of the bowel and preventive antibiotics are the primary means whereby this can be accomplished.

The importance of intestinal antisepsis as a component of bowel preparation for colon resection has been confirmed by numerous studies. Equally important, however, is mechanical preparation of the bowel to remove as much of the fecal material as possible. Many effective regimens have been suggested. Ours is essentially the same as that recommended by Condon:[22,23]

TABLE 6. INDICATIONS FOR STAGING OR
PROXIMAL DIVERSION.[21]

Systemic factors:	
Severe associated trauma and blood loss	+ +
Recent shock	+
Uremia	Variable with degree
Diabetes (mild 0 moderate + severe + +)	Variable with degree
Protein depletion - 20% weight loss (Can be mitigated with preoperative hyperalimentation)	+
Advanced age	+
Emergency operation	+
Radiation (curative doses >6 weeks prior)	+

1. Clear liquid diet beginning on day 1.
2. Oral magnesium citrate, 12 oz. at 1:00 PM on day 1.
3. Saline enema at bedtime on day 1.
4. Oral magnesium citrate, 12 oz. at 1:00 PM on day 2.
5. One gram each of neomycin and erythromycin base at 1:00 PM, 2:00 PM, and 11:00 PM on day 2.
6. Operation on day 3.

The value of preventive antibiotics in high risk procedures has been demonstrated in numerous prospective studies. These studies have also indicated that the specific antibiotic used is of much less consequence than the timing of its administration. The seminal work of Burke et al. showed that there is a decisive period of three to four hours following the seeding of tissue with bacteria during which an infection starts. Further, this work shows that if an appropriate antibiotic is present in the tissue at the time the seeding takes place, the infection will most likely be aborted. However, if the antibiotic reaches the tissue after that decisive period, its effectiveness is substantially less. Therefore, preventive antibiotics should be administered, starting at no more than two hours before the operation, and appropriate tissue level should be maintained approximately four hours following the end of the operation (Figure 6).[7]

The combination of thorough bowel preparation and the appropriate administration of preventive antibiotics has been a major

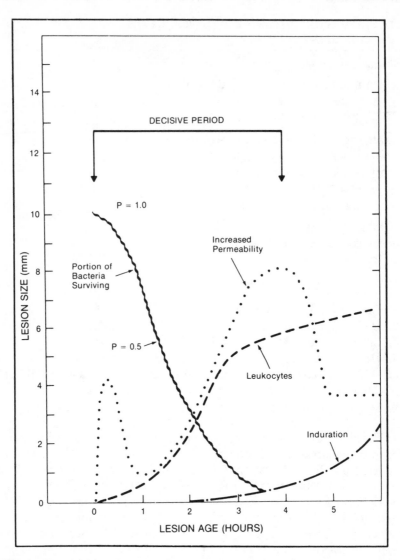

FIG. 6. The period of active tissue antibacterial activity (decisive period) compared with the arrival of leukocytes in the tissue, the beginning of induration, and the phases of vascular permeability. (After Leak LV, Burke JF. In Zweifach BW, Grant L, McClusky RR (eds.) The Inflammatory Response, Vol III, 2nd ed. New York, Academic Press, 1974.)

factor in reducing morbidity rates and the incidence of anastomotic leaks in recent years following colonic resection procedures.

One must caution, however, that once before in the history of surgery, surgeons substituted antibiotics for sound judgment and good technique, and many patients suffered. Well used antibiotics *are* helpful; but sound judgment, good technique and adequate supportive care are at least as equally as important.

CONCLUSIONS

Anastomotic leakage and infection are both commonplace after colonic resection procedures. The question of whether infection causes leakage, or leakage results in infection, is still moot, much as "which came first, the chicken or the egg?" From a practical, clinical point of view, it is not necessary that this question be answered insofar as the management of individual patients is concerned, because these two phenomena are so closely interrelated. What is important is the recognition and management of the risk factors that predispose such patients to both leakage *and* infection. Underlying the prevention of morbidity in patients undergoing colonic resection is the restoration and maintenance of adequate nutrition, blood volume, and tissue perfusion so that host defenses can function at optimal levels; and effective preparation of the bowel along with the administration of preventive antibiotics to preclude the establishment of infection during the decisive period. Here lies the road to further reduction of the infection and leakage rates that accompany colonic resection with primary anastomosis.

REFERENCES

1. Hawley PR, et al.: The etiology of colonic anastomotic leaks. Proc R Soc Med 63:28, 1970.
2. Irvin TT, Hunt TK: Pathogenesis and prevention of disruption of colonic anastomoses in traumatized rats. Br J. Surg 61:437, 1974.
3. Irvin TT, Hunt TK: The effect of trauma on colonic healing. Br J Surg 61:430, 1974.
4. Irvin TT, Hunt TK: Effect of malnutrition on colonic healing. Ann Surg 180:765, 1974.
5. Irvin TT, Hunt TK: Reappraisal of the healing process of anastomoses of the colon. Surg Gynec Obstet 138:741, 1974.
6. Hawley PR et al.: Collagenase activity in the gastrointestinal tract. Br J Surg 57:61, 1970.

7. Hunt TK, Dunphy JE (eds.): Fundamentals of Wound Management. New York, Appleton-Century-Crofts, 1979.
8. Hunt TK (ed.): Wound Healing and Wound Infection: Theory and Surgical Practice, New York, Appleton-Century-Crofts, 1980.
9. Schrock TR, Deveney CW, Dunphy JE: Factors contributing to leakage of colonic anastomoses. Ann Surg 197:513, 1973.
10. Pai MP, Hunt TK: Effect of varying oxygen tensions on healing of open sounds. Surg Gynec Obstet 135:756, 1972.
11. Stephens FO, Hunt TK: Effect of changes in inspired oxygen and carbon dioxide tensions on wound tensile strength: An experimental study. Ann Surg 173:515, 1971.
12. Chang N, Goodson WH III, Gottrup F, Hunt TK: Direct measurement of tissue oxygen tension in postoperative patients. (Submitted for publication.)
13. Hunt TK, Conolly WB, Aronson SB, Goldstein P: Anaerobic metabolism and wound healing: An hypothesis for the initiation and cessation of collagen synthesis in wounds. Am J Surg 135:328−332, 1978.
14. Hunt TK et al.: Oxygen tension and wound infection. Surg Forum 23:47, 1972.
15. Hunt TK, et al.: The effect of differing ambient oxygen tensions on wound infection. Ann Surg 181:35, 1975.
16. Niinikoski J, et al.: Respiratory gas tensions and collagen in infected wounds. Ann Surg 175:588, 1972.
17. Hunt TK, et al.: Oxygen in wound healing enhancement: Cellular effects of oxygen. In Hyperbaric Oxygen Therapy, JC Davis, TK Hunt (eds.), Bethesda, Maryland, Undersea Medical Society, 1977.
18. Hohn DC, et al.: Effect of O_2 tension on microbicidal function of leukocytes in wounds and in vitro. Surg Forum 27:18, 1976.
19. Ravitch MM, Brolin R, Kolter J, Yap S: Studies in the healing of intestinal anastomoses. World J Surg 5:4 627−637, July, 1981.
20. Heughan et al.: The effect of anemia on wound healing. Ann Surg 179:163, 1974.
21. Morgenstern L, Yamakawa T, Ben-Shoshan M, Lippman H: Anastomotic leakage after low colonic anastomosis: Clinical and experimental aspects. Am J Surg 123:104−109, Jan, 1972.
22. Nichols RL, Broido P, Condon RE, et al.: Effect of preoperative neomycin-erythromycin intestinal preparation on the incidence of infectious complications following colon surgery. Ann Surg 178:453, 1973.
23. Clarke JS, Condon RE, Bartlett JG, et al.: Preoperative oral antibiotics reduce septic complications of colored operations: Results of prospective randomized double-blind clinical study. Ann Surg 186:251, 1977.

Discussion

DR. SIMMONS: Dr. Bartlett, what antibiotics do you use for patients with peritonitis nowadays? What's your first choice of drugs and why?

DR. BARTLETT: We always use a combination of drugs for fecal peritonitis. We use an aminoglycoside. I prefer either tobramycin or gentamicin, though I'd rather not get into a discussion of the relative merits of those two drugs. The second drug would be clindamycin, metronidazole, or cefoxitin. I generally serve as a consultant; these are the drugs that are already being used in most instances, and these are the ones which I would endorse. If the patient does not respond, my experience is that it's generally due to one of three causes: (1) failure to recognize undrained pus, which may not be readily apparent; (2) the infection has progressed too far in its natural evolution to show a demonstrable response to antibiotics (for example, people still die of pneumococcal pneumonia despite therapy with penicillin); (3) the infection is caused by an organism which is not included in our antibiotic regimen. The last is relatively uncommon with the broad spectrum combinations in common usage. Occasional cases will involve an unusually resistant negative rod which is unusual in peritonitis. Another possibility is the enterococcus. None of the regimens mentioned here would be considered optimal for the enterococcus and that would become a consideration. We would probably treat the enterococcus initially if it was present in the blood stream; ampicillin or penicillin combined with an aminoglycoside would be appropriate for this organism.

DR. STONE: We have had a high incidence of renal failure from aminoglycoside use. If you administer these drugs to patients who have renal ischemia, be it from severe dehydration or trauma, the incidence of renal failure is quite high, so we try to avoid the use of aminoglycosides and instead use a second or third generation cephalosporin antimicrobial agent for the aerobic component. Certain of these have a good anaerobic spectrum and accordingly they can be used alone; but others are not sufficiently reliable against anaerobes, and where recurrent sepsis is suspected one would want to add another agent. There's not a great deal of difference in the test tube, depending upon how you test them, between clindamycin, erythromycin, and metronidazole; but as far as pharmacology is concerned, probably metronidazole has the best tissue penetration and that would probably be the first choice followed by erythromycin and then clindamycin. Basically we prefer to use a second or third generation cephalosporin for the aerobic organisms and, in certain settings, metronidazole or clindamycin for the anaerobes.

DR. NICHOLS: The incidence of aminoglycoside toxicity including renal involvement can be greatly minimized by attention to two primary points: (1) monitoring the serum levels of the aminoglycoside and (2) limiting the therapy to ten days or less. I would agree with Dr. Stone regarding the efficacy of metronidazole and clindamycin in anaerobic infections. However, erythromycin is rarely indicated in the systemic treatment of anaerobic infections due to the high incidence of local phlebitis and, more importantly, due to the possibility of inactivation of the erythromycin in acidic (low pH) septic focuses. Additional prospective blinded clinical studies are now indicated to compare cefoxitin and moxalactam with combination therapy in established polymicrobial infection in the surgical patient.

DR. BARTLETT: I want to make sure the audience understands what is meant by the terms first, second, and third generation cephalosporins. First generation is everything before November, 1979. The principal drugs in that group, all of which have identical spectra of activity, are cephaloridine, cefazolin, and cephalothin. In November, 1979, we got the second generation, including cefoxitin and cefamandole. The third generation includes drugs such as recently marketed cefotaxime and moxalactum. The second generation cephalosporins have a somewhat expanded spectrum of activity, and the third generation drugs have an even greater spectrum. Those are the ones that Dr. Stone is talking about. Quite frankly, of all the drugs I've just mentioned, I really think there are only two that can be viewed as good agents against *Bacteroides fragilis*. One is cefoxitin and the other is moxalactum.

DR. STONE: I'd like to add just one word to that. The preventive use of antibiotics is quite different. I see a lot of people using gentamicin and tobramycin for IV prevention in addition to bowel prep, and the ratio of danger to gain is very high. I personally don't do that.

DR. SIMMONS: The aminoglycoside toxicity problem is very real. My impression, however, is that the major error with aminoglycosides is insufficient dosage. Do you think that's true? Do you think the toxicity is serious and irreversible? What is the need for doing levels on patients who are getting an aminoglycoside?

DR. BARTLETT: I agree with you that the error tends to be on the low side. There is a tendency to use 80 mg every 8 hours for all patients. The dosage we use is 1.7 mg per kg in a patient with normal renal function, and we either modify the dose or the dosing interval for patients that have renal failure. We generally obtain peak and valley levels, a peak at 45 minutes after infusion and a valley just before the next infusion, in patients who have a complicated medical condition or who are receiving the drug for an extended period. Almost anybody with intraabdominal sepsis would qualify. We would probably obtain that level on the third day of therapy. We want a peak between four and eight mg/ml and we want a valley of less than two mg/ml. Those are the general guidelines we use. When we've followed this regimen, we have found that in virtually all patients the nephrotoxicity, as described by an increase in serum creatinine, will be reversible. The tubular damage, similar to acute tubular necrosis, recovers. It is only the patient who is grossly neglected that gets overt irreversible renal failure with aminoglycosides. I've never seen that unless there is simply no monitoring of antibiotic level and serum creatinine during the course of treatment. One exception is with the simultaneous administration of ethacrynic acid. The concurrent use of these two drugs should be avoided.

DR. SIMMONS: Dr. Bjornson, frequently, you'll be treating a patient with what seems to be a good empiric choice of antibiotics and the fever either doesn't go away or recurs. What are your indications for changing the antibiotics in intraabdominal sepsis, and what do you change to?

DR. BJORNSON: This is a very frequent problem. First of all, I hope that the surgeon who operated on the patient obtained appropriate cultures intraoperatively so we have a rational basis on which to change our antibiotic therapy.

DR. SIMMONS: The first cultures came back as *E. coli, Klebsiella, B. fragilis,* with unidentified organisms to be identified later.

DR. BJORNSON: The *E. coli* and *Klebsiella* are probably going to be sensitive to gentamicin and hopefully that will take care of the mixed infection. About 10+% of *B. fragilis* are resistant to clindamycin and a slightly lower percent has been shown to be resistant to metronidazole, though extensive experience isn't available with this drug. I'd first suspect an undrained collection of pus as the most likely cause of the persistent fever and leukocytosis. I'd consider adding penicillin to the therapeutic regimen because there are some penicillin-sensitive anaerobes, especially the anaerobic cocci, whose role in synergistic mixed infections is poorly understood. In other words, I'd check the cultures and look for another problem before changing antibiotics.

DR. SIMMONS: Dr. Stone, do you have a different approach to that problem? I think it's the most common one we're faced with as surgical infectious disease consultants.

DR. STONE: If the patient has been on a given antibiotic regimen for less than two days, I would not change it; if the patient has been on an antibiotic regimen for more than five days, I would change it. However, as has been mentioned, it is so important to determine whether there is some other source such as undrained or poorly drained pus. We've had a number of patients with abscesses that have been drained but have continued to drain profusely; and a profusely draining abscess several days following the operative procedure performed to gain drainage is an abscess that's poorly drained, and it requires more dependent or better drainage. Often times all one needs to do is turn the patient prone and a fever of

39C will become normal as a result of dependent drainage. It is in this setting that often times a sinogram is useful if there is an established tract. A crosstable lateral film in conjunction with the sinogram helps. We look for an abscess that has not yet been identified and drained. Most of our patients have good antibiotic coverage for everything except enterococcus and we would be suspicious of enterococcus participating in this setting so we would add ampicillin to the regimen. We would not change anything else. If the patient is allergic to penicillin, we would possibly use vancomycin. If this patient had been on antimicrobial therapy for a prolonged period, that is for seven to ten days, we would be suspicious of an overgrowth of yeast. Accordingly, we would then check arterial blood cultures to see if there has been yeast invasion. It is important to use arterial, not venous, cultures, because they are much more reliable. We would also look in the urine for yeast. If the patient has a candidemia rather than a bacteremia, then they will have yeast in the urine; if they don't there will be no yeast in the urine, and it aids you in differentiating between the two. So we would look for other avenues, other sources; not just within the abdomen but in the lungs, the GI tract, possibly in the urinary tract for an obstruction. It is just a matter of sorting through things. Changing the antibiotic is important only to gain a little time until you identify the other source.

DR. SIMMONS: Dr. Bartlett, the fourth day *Candida* is reported by the laboratory. The patient is doing well on antibacterial therapy. Do you change therapy to treat the *Candida* which is co-existent? How about for *Pseudomonas* if it were reported late?

DR. BARTLETT: I rarely, as a general rule, change antibiotics on the basis of a bacteriology report if the patient is doing well. With *Candida,* the answer is a little bit easier because the required drug is one that we would avoid unless we were actually forced to use it. If the *Candida* was recovered from the original specimen, I wouldn't worry about it as much as if it were recovered from a subsequent arterial blood culture as described by Dr. Stone. *Pseudomonas aeruginosa* is easier to attack. If, for example, it was sensitive to one aminoglycoside and I was using another, I would just change the aminoglycoside. If it meant adding an aminoglycoside, and there was a reason for avoiding aminoglycosides, I would not do so if the patient was doing well. In other words, I would not alter my antibiotic regimen simply because an organism was found at the original site of infection which was not covered initially. This would apply especially to polymicrobial infections. If it was a single species recovered in pure culture, I'd probably feel differently.

DR. SIMMONS: I find the laboratory useless most of the time in polymicrobial intraperitoneal sepsis. They tell you what you don't have, not what you do have; and if you pay too much attention to it you end up changing drugs when you have already chosen, by empiric or statistical means, the best therapy. We feel that you should treat the enterococcus because in our series we have had a large number of enterococcus breakthroughs in patients who didn't receive ampicillin as one of the initial drug combination. On the other hand, we have never had an enterococcus breakthrough when we've used ampicillin at all, and it's such a benign drug to use. Now a week has passed and you really do have evidence of an intraabdominal abscess. Dr. Hunt, with the patient having been on clindamycin and gentamicin all this time, is there any reason to switch to metronidazole?

DR. HUNT: If the patient had not been on clindamycin you would want to add metronidazole at this point because the statistics are that that patient would have an anaerobic infection. I don't usually change from clindamycin to metronidazole; rather I look for the abscess and try to drain it surgically. If bacteremia were identified by means of serial blood cultures, I would treat it; and if metronidazole turned out marginally superior, I would not be afraid to change from clindamycin.

DR. SIMMONS: There's some talk in infectious disease circles that metronidazole has become the treatment of choice, because of its penetration, for deep-seated abscesses that are presumed to have an anaerobic component. Would you comment, Dr. Bartlett?

DR. BARTLETT: I think in the test tube metronidazole is a superior drug; and in the animal models this has also now been demonstrated. I think that there is probably no drug that could be considered the equivalent or better than metronidazole from the currently available pharmacopeia. However, our clinical experience has been that clindamycin, cefoxitin, metronidazole, and a number of other drugs that have been mentioned are perhaps equally meritorius in all the comparative trials that have been done. I think I would change to metronidazole in the patient that you just mentioned if he had persistent *Bacteroides fragilis* bacteremia. But an abscess needs to be drained; that's not a problem with the antibiotic, rather it's a problem of undrained pus.

DR. SIMMONS: Under what circumstances would you add amphotericin, other than for persistent candidemia?

DR. BARTLETT: For retinal disease due to *Candida*. This is potentially lethal and blinding; and for that matter, I treat any seriously degenerating patient in whom I can get silver stains showing the presence of *Candida* in tissue. Ordinarily these chronic *Candida* problems are mainly a matter of getting a patient better nourished, giving him some time, and taking care of him rather than giving amphotericin.

DR. SIMMONS: In our experience, intraabdominal *Candida* can be an occasional serious problem, especially after upper intestinal or gastric perforations; and we don't hesitate to use amphotericin. You don't *have* to treat such patients with the same dosage you might use for histoplasmosis or cryptococcosis. When *Candida* is present in the peritoneal cavity, you generally treat it for a fairly brief period of time.

DR. STONE: There are just a few areas which *Candida* can and will invade. Obviously if it colonizes an indwelling intravenous line, that's direct invasion; but it can invade across the mucous membrane of the proximal small bowel, just passively going across it and getting into the lymphatics; and it can invade across a serosal membrane; but it is very difficult for *Candida* to invade via granulating tissue. The peritoneum is an ideal membrane for *Candida* to penetrate and cause a candidemia. We would not produce *Candida* infection of the blood stream, nor persistence of *Candida*, when we created sterile abscesses or when we injected huge amounts of *Candida* directly into muscle, subcutaneous spaces or other organs of dogs and monkeys. So the particularr aspect that Dr. Simmons refers to, that of *Candida* participating in peritonitis, can be a most important issue.

DR. BJORNSON: The decision to initiate amphotericin B therapy for *Candida* is a major problem for us, because of the difficulty in documenting invasive infection cause by *Candida*. The criteria which we use for starting amphotericin B therapy are persistent candidemia and *Candida endophthalmitis.* Rising antibody titers have been helpful in a minority of our patients with presumed invasive candidiasis.

DR. SIMMONS: Dr. Hunt, would you comment on the recently reported experience with percutaneous drainage of intraabdominal abscesses?

DR. HUNT: This is a technique that has been quick to catch on because nobody likes to drain abscesses. They did have a mortality rate in that series. It was small, but significant; and one wonders whether those deaths represented patients who would have died anyway or ones who might have survived if they'd had their abscesses drained widely. I have had a lot of experience with abscesses that have a little nick put in them and a drain inserted; yet these patients continue to be febrile. So I'm rather doubtful that this technique can be applied generally. There may be a place for it in draining a chronic abscess, or in patients who aren't very sick. I just did one a few weeks ago in a Jehovah's Witness with a hematocrit of 13, hemorrhagic pancreatitis, and a pseudocyst of the pancreas. There wasn't much choice in this patient and it worked beautifully for a while. She didn't become septic for a valuable few weeks. But in time we had to drain widely. However, I think you have to be careful. We've had a number of patients who have had the catheters put in and been over vigorously irrigated who have had septic episodes. My preference is still for surgical drainage of all abscesses that can be drained surgically.

DR. NICHOLS: The use of percutaneous needle aspiration of intraabdominal abscesses requires precise technique and a close working relationship between the radiologist and the surgeon. If this is available the technique can be very helpful, especially in the critically ill patient with a solitary intraabdominal abscess.

DR. STONE: Many intraperitoneal abscesses will spontaneously drain into the GI tract. You can note the scar where the abscess was if you re-explore such a patient at a subsequent date because of mechanical intestinal obstruction.

DR. SIMMONS: In the treatment of really severe peritonitis, how do you feel about peritoneal debridement? How radical should you be? What holes, what spaces, or potential spaces should you open up? Which ones should you avoid opening up? Assume a perforated appendicitis in a 75-year-old man. It's reasonably well localized to the pelvis. Where else should you go, if anywhere, and what should you do there?

DR. BJORNSON: I would drain it locally, because the more you go routing around in the abdomen, the more likely you are to spread infection to other areas of the abdomen which are not initially involved. I would institute appropriate drainage of the local area and debride as much of the purulent material as is feasible in the initial operative procedure.

DR. SIMMONS: Assume perforated diverticulitis in the same man. Everything is clearly involved except above the liver and maybe the lesser sac. What do you do then? Do you go above the liver? Do you go into the lesser sac?

DR. HUNT: I think that there's an important point here. When you first open an abdomen with a perforated viscus, you have your best opportunity to determine the source. I frequently see residents open the abdomen in a hurry and then plunge their hand down toward where they think the pus is going to come from, trying to see if their diagnosis is correct; and by the time they've dragged out a loop of bowel or something, you're not quite sure where the infection came from, what its pattern is, or how well it's localized. I start looking around at those spaces immediately upon opening, and if early in the operation I think they aren't seriously contaminated, if I think there's no vegetable material in there, I have made a point of not going after them, I have rarely been sorry. However, if there is vegetable material or foreign body sitting up above the liver, you've got to go after it and get it out. On some cases when there's a very thick shaggy fibrin on the bowel, I'll even try to wipe it off, but there I really practice what I preached in my sermon. I believe that in such cases you should redouble your efforts to increase your patient's resistance. In the long run, this is more effective than doing anything except taking out foreign bodies.

DR. SIMMONS: Dr. Stone, would you address the problems of draining the peritoneal cavity?

DR. STONE: First, the inflammatory process lies somewhere between four and six days, and has reached the stage where the fibrin adhesions are being vascularized. If you go pawing about the peritoneal cavity beyond the fifth or sixth day, you frequently disrupt all of this vascular adhesion and the patient has a great deal of bleeding. This complicates the problem as has been detailed by Dr. Simmons. Second, you are very likely to get into the bowel, with the consequence that you can't sew it closed, and you're going to have to exteriorize the bowel. So, if upon entry one finds very vascularized adhesions, i.e., a process that's somewhere beyond the fourth or fifth day, often times you elect not to proceed with this dissection. Third is the question of what is adequate debridement in the patient with diverticulitis? Is it resection of the segment of colon and bringing out an end stoma, as in appendicitis that includes appendectomy? We don't know. We are randomizing that right now trying to find out whether one should go ahead and resect the bowel or not. There's a lot of testimony in the literature one way and the other. Fourth, when you put drains in all these pockets, I don't think you do anything but add foreign body, and that seems to increase the problem of infection. I have not been convinced that I can drain the whole peritoneal cavity. If it's an isolated single abscess, then I believe one can drain it well; but drains in a generalized process all seem to wall off and each drains a little tiny spot. The only way around this would be to introduce hundreds of drains in the peritoneal cavity and let the patient look like they've got a belly that's a brush!

DR. HUNT: I tend to agree with you, but there are a few exceptions. One is in rectal injuries. The likelihood of a pelvic abscess is so great that the efficacy of drains has been well demonstrated. The debridement then will often include a rectal washout, too, which we haven't mentioned.

DR. SIMMONS: Dr. Stone, you have studied the problems of the perforated rectum; what do you do in such cases?

DR. STONE: If a patient has a perforated rectum, he has a divided colostomy. We tend to oversew the end and drop it back in the abdomen. Following that we put in a retrorectal drain, primarily to spread the levator sling. It's amazing how rapidly a mixed flora infection will dissect in the loose areolar tissue of the retroperitoneum. It will dissect much more rapidly than it will transperitoneally, and it's incredible how fast it goes. We do something to spread the levator sling so if there is a beginning dissection retroperitoneally, just the gas pressure within will have flooded our mechanism out. We assume that's what it is, but it's not proven.

DR. SIMMONS: Dr. Hunt, is there anything we can do to make wounds heal better?

DR. HUNT: You can fix specific defects nutritionally; and our data suggest that if you can provide a little bit of hyperoxygenation, an arterial PO_2 of 150 in a well-perfused patient, you can speed it a bit. That's about all.

DR. SIMMONS: Is there any role for immediate prep of the colon in unprepped bowel by putting an iodophor solution into the lumen and sterilizing it before you do the anastamosis?

DR. NICHOLS: In our hands, this technique has been a messy affair. Although experimental data is available demonstrating the microbiologic efficacy of the "Instant Bowel Prep" with iodophor solutions, clinical studies proving this point are not available in this setting. We still rely on appropriate intravenous polymicrobial coverage in addition to meticulous surgical technique.

DR. HUNT: In some cases, if you open the bowel and you find it isn't as well prepped as you had hoped, and you've got stool oozing out, it's reasonable to wash it out with something that's bactericidal. Certainly in the case of a rectal injury, rather than leave a column of stool lying on a complex suture line you want to get that out. But no, I haven't made a point of trying to wash the bowel out extensively; I just try to keep from contaminating the peritoneum.

Index

I

infections, role of anaerobes in, 27–44
intraabdominal abscess, 49–60
intraoperative transfusion as risk factor, 102
intraperitoneal abscess, prevention of, 19–22
intravenous feeding, 13
iodophor solution, 117

K

KDO (2-keto-3-deoxy-octonate), 71
Klebsiella, 110

L

lactobacilli, 9
leak, anastomotic, 89–105
levator sling, 116
lipopolysaccharide (LPS), 70–72
LPS (see lipopolysaccharide)
lysis, collagen, 90–96

M

macrophages, 94
mesothelium, 4, 6
metronidazole, 15–16, 56–60, 86, 107, 112
microflora, endogenous, 28–31, 49–60
midabdominal abscess, 85
model, animal, 66–67
   rat, 51–54
moxalactam, 56–57, 109

O

operation in peritonitis, 16–19
outer membrane complex (OMC), 70–72
oxygen, 97–99

P

pelvis abscess, 84
penicillin, 108
perforated appendicitis, 32–35
perforation, colon, 79–81
peritoneal cavity, physiology of, 2–6
peritonitis, 1–22, 34–35
physiology of peritoneal cavity, 2–6
PMNs (see polymorphonuclear leukocytes)
polymorphonuclear leukocytes (PMNs), 72–73, 94
preoperative treatment of peritonitis, 13
primary peritonitis, 1
Pseudomonas aeruginosa, 111

R

radiation as a risk factor, 101
recurrent sepsis, 79–87
risk factors in anastomosis, 100–102

S

Salmonella enteritidis, 70
S. aureus, 58–59, 66
secondary peritonitis, 1–2
sepsis, recurrent, 79–87
starvation, 96
steroids, 96–97
streptococci, 9–10
subphrenic abscess, 85
synergy, bacterial, 65–73
synthesis, collagen, 96–99

T

tobramycin, 107, 109
transfusion, intraoperative, 102